Manife

The Ultimate Guide to Creating the Life of Your Dreams

Inspirational Stories
of Personal Empowerment,
Courage and Success

Compiled by
Debbi Chambers

ISBN: 978-1-934919-04-0 / 1-934919-04-7

More Heart Than Talent Publishing, Inc.

6507 Pacific Ave #329
Stockton, CA 95207 USA
Toll Free: 800-208-2260
www.MHTPublishing.com

FAX: 209-467-3260

Cover art by FlowMotion Inc.

Printed in the United States of America

This book is dedicated to my parents, Patrick and Darlene. Without their collaboration and co-creation, I would not be here, experiencing this fantastic adventure called "Life".

Manifest Success

In Appreciation

I am grateful to be blessed and surrounded by the love and support of family, friends and mentors. I live in a constant state of gratitude and awe that allows me to reap the harvest that manifests from this vibration. Thank you for your strength, energy and support. You inspire me daily.

I am honored to exchange a spiritual, heart-felt hug of gratitude with each of our authors. These special souls felt compelled to seize this opportunity to share their personal stories in the spirit of serving and assisting others on their journey.

Foreword

I believe that everyone has a message within them that could greatly impact others, but many do not have access to the proper tools and resources to deliver this message. Debbi's project, *Manifest Success: The Ultimate Guide to Creating the Life of Your Dreams,* has created an opportunity for a select group authors to achieve the credibility of being published alongside already successful and established authors, combined with a powerful marketing program to bring their brilliance to the world.

I have seen Debbi flourish in her brilliance, bringing tremendous value to others through her powerful ideas and creativity during the last few years. She has personally raced along the path to success and knows from personal experience how much easier it is to manifest the success we all seek rather than continue to struggle. It is her experience through her journey that inspired her to create this collaborative book, celebrating the success of others, in order to assist you in your journey. Regardless of what success means to you personally, there is a message for you inside this book that will touch your soul and inspire you to greatness.

If you have been seeking insight and wisdom from people just like you to assist you through your journey, I urge you to turn the page and experience the powerful truth and insight of these true stories from those who have been there, done that, and manifested their own success.

You are a Masterpiece in progress, follow the insight inside this book and remember, this is *The Ultimate Guide to Creating the Life of Your Dreams!*

Erica Combs
President, More Heart Than Talent Publishing, Inc.
www.mhtpublishing.com

Table of Contents

Table of Contents

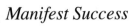

Expectations Expand Your Comfort Zone

Once upon a time, I had this great, outstanding, incredible, passionate, all encompassing, amazingly powerful desire, but I didn't *expect* it to really happen, and therefore…I was right.

You can dream, you can desire, you can be positive about your goals all you want, but if you do not *expect* or truly believe that change will happen, it is highly unlikely that you will achieve your goal. Your expectations must coincide with your outcomes.

Don't Let Your Past Dictate Your Future

Let's look for a moment at a person that faithfully makes a New Year's resolution. (I'll use a monetary example here, simply because it will be more easily measured and imagined, but this lesson about expectations can and should be used in all areas of your life.) For five years that individual has made the same resolution – that he will be out of credit card debt by the end of the year and have total financial abundance. Each year, this person finds himself in the same place, or worse, he is even further in debt, only to make the same resolution the following year. No matter how strong the desire, if the subconscious mind expects failure, based on past results, one receives what one expects. Doubt, fear, and negative expectations based on past results will not lead to abundance.

Just like you cannot be truly grateful and unhappy at the same time, you cannot *expect* financial abundance and mediocrity at the same time. You must live in one expectation or the other. How is this accomplished? The answer is not complicated: *You cannot let the past dictate your future.*

Living in the past is counterproductive. It has no bearing on your future results. If you desire financial abundance but expect failure based on past results, you are living in the wrong parameter of your mind. The past tells you exactly where you are. Do you know where you want to be? Visualize your future. Run your own personal movie of what you want to have or be. Bring your mind into the present. Visualize that abundance as though it is already yours, *today*. Put the past where it belongs...behind you. Your future cannot be dictated by your past if you do not allow it to be.

Any personal development or law of attraction study will teach you that *the past does not equal the future.* If you have made the choice to leave the past where it belongs, behind you, then your present and future become wide open to accept the reality that you can *expect* anything you desire. The past created the outcome of where you are today. It has no bearing on where you will be or what you can achieve in the future if you can accept this law.

Be Grateful Now

Gratitude, the ability to be truly thankful for what you have today, will help you live in the present. When the plane's going down, no one is an atheist. Don't wait until you're about to crash to be grateful. Be grateful *now* for your present condition, and *expect* your future to be rewarding and abundant based on your new attitude and the positive actions you are taking to reach that abundance.

Expectation can be a very powerful tool in your arsenal of success if you live in the present and visualize your dreams as if they are yours right now. Those visualizations will turn into realities as long as you leave your past failures out of the equation.

There is no substitute for positive action. Neither positive thought nor endless affirmations can replace taking positive steps towards your goals. Read the books, visualize your dreams and goals, begin to think the way a successful person thinks, behave the way a financially abundant person behaves, and you will cease dwelling on past failures, move your thoughts to the present and your abundant future, and begin to *Always Expect Success*.

Beyond the Comfort Zone

As we all know, doing the same thing over and over again *expecting* different results is the definition of insanity. This leads me to one of the most rewarding aspects of growth on your path to freedom, the ability to step beyond your comfort zone.

Any successful person you see, at some point has stepped beyond their initial comfort zone. We all start in the same place. We were all infants, teens, and young adults. At some point, some of us chose to stay where we are, and others chose to step beyond, into the unknown, breaking through their existing comfort zone.

This is another area of growth where you cannot have both. You cannot remain complacent, unwilling to grow, expand or take risks, and expect to achieve greater results in your life. No matter what aspect of life you are contemplating, in order to see change you must step up to the plate and take a swing. Even when you miss, you are still expanding your circle of influence simply by taking some form of positive action.

Stepping outside of your comfort zone – taking an action that makes you uncomfortable in order to achieve a positive result – appears on the surface to be one of the most difficult challenges. It is much easier to continue doing what you have always done to get by, even if you are uncomfortable financially, spiritually, or otherwise. Change always feels uncomfortable, which is why so many people live in mediocrity. Even

15

when people are experiencing lack financially, in business or personal success, or even in a personal relationship, the thought of changing scares them into living with mediocrity; in other words, they are comfortable. Change means risk, and we can't have that!

Fear of living outside of your comfort zone means missing out on one of the greatest thrills in life. So often, what seemed so difficult in your mind turns out to be exceptionally rewarding and even fun when you have completed the task. Risk is a positive term – not a negative term, as we have often believed. If you are in sales, the act of taking a risk and speaking to that CEO you are afraid to approach could be the most rewarding experience of your business. It could lead to contacts and growth beyond your imagination. What's the worst-case scenario? A "No"? You are now one step closer to achieving a positive "Yes" with the next CEO. The alternative is to do nothing, remain in your current position, dream about the possibilities, continue doing what you have done in the past, and *hope* things will get better.

Jim Rohn states, "Don't wish things were easier; wish you were better. Don't wish for fewer problems; wish for better skills." The only path to better skills is to expand your comfort zone. Building new skills may still feel uncomfortable, but now you understand that it may be a necessary step if you *expect* to match your goals. As you continue to challenge yourself, take chances, and try new things, the more you will grow and build a rewarding future. Ultimately, the things you consider a risk will become second nature. You will be moving forward three or four steps beyond your initial risk factor. Imagine the rewards!

Make Sure Your Goals and Choices Match

If your goal is financial abundance and you are currently living with financial lack, then you must make choices that are consistent with your goals. The choices you have made in the past have left you with the mediocrity you are currently experiencing. You are in a constant comfort zone that is not assisting you. Make choices that match your goal. Step out of your current comfort zone and take action to expand your influence. Speak to another successful person, copy their actions and results, read personal development books, and put in the extra effort that places you above the rest. Do the things that the members in your current surroundings cannot or will not do. Be willing to step into unfamiliar territory. Forget the fear and focus on the positive outcome.

When you *turn your business on* in the morning, does your business *return the favor*? Step out of your comfort zone, experience the excitement, *expect* the growth, and enjoy the ride. It's *your* choice – *you* decide. *Always Expect Success!*

Marcus Abbott resides on the shoreline of Connecticut. He is a national award-winning designer in professional theater, music, and film. He is a successful entrepreneur and trainer, implementing powerful personal development and mentoring techniques. Marcus believes that the combination of proactive personal development, a lucrative financial vehicle, and effective partnering with like-minded people is a recipe for success. Marcus maintains a sincere desire to assist others. He lives by the adage *"Always Expect Success!"*. **For more information, visit www. MarcusAbott.com or www.PlatinumTravelSolutions.com.**

Manifest Success

Beverly Ameykeller

An Old Oak Tree's Message
"I Am That, I Am"

Listen, Learn, and Grow with the Experience

Though I have always been aware of nature, with today's fast pace I had to be reminded to "stop and smell the roses"…not just slow down, but rather become one with the present, become one with nature. (Quite honestly, I don't know whether this newly acquired trait of actually being in the "now" manifested in the usual "twenty-one days to have a change become a habit" or rather that it was through a very loud and clear message from an old oak tree with whom I had previously not given the time of day. I suspect it's been the later.) Where I once believed that to "stop and smell the roses" meant just that…literally to grab a few seconds of time and allow my eyes a glimpse and my nose a sniff, I've learned that it really means so much more; it's about *being in nature and nature being in us, teaching us profound messages* as we take the time to really listen, learn, and grow with the experience.

The Way of Progress

I had an experience with an old oak tree recently that was the catalyst for learning nature's special message in my own life. The shingles on our house had reached their limits, and when water began dripping from our ceilings and creating puddles on the floor, we decided to install a new roof. (It didn't take much thinking to reach this conclusion!) We went through the usual process of getting roofing estimates, selecting the best company, obtaining the necessary permits, and removing the old roof and installing

19

the new one. Total left-brain thinking: make a decision, create action, and get a result. Somewhere in this step-by-step procedure, it occurred to all involved that a rather large oak tree was impeding the speed of the project. The tree's branches were *almost* touching the roof and probably had for years. The large limbs were cascading over the driveway and acorns were everywhere, unnoticed until now.

One obscure oak tree couldn't stand in the way of progress, now could it? Left-brain *thinking* quickly assessed the cost and time factors to remove limbs verses the entire tree, and the unanimous vote was to **remove the tree**! (I was personally involved in this hasty decision, and even now, I regret it.) But how could just one oak tree make any difference? The mere size of the project overshadowed the size of the tree, so the decision appeared to be the right one. (The decision was made with thought – just not with feelings.) Time did not permit any of us decision makers a minute to reflect on the fact that the tree had been in existence long before the idea of a housing development was conceived and, for that matter, long before our home was built. No, not one of us took a moment to reflect on the contributions the oak tree had made...shade, a natural coolant, oxygen for the planet, natural environments and habitats for birds, butterflies, armadillos, insects, and squirrels – not to mention those annoying, driveway-staining acorns being a food source, especially for those squirrels! Time was of the essence...how many days, or hours or minutes before it might rain, or the roofers would have to move on to another job, or more codes would be passed and more restructuring would be required? No time to "stop and smell the roses" here! No time to become one with the present (the environment, that oak tree), no being one with nature! With a thunderous crash, the oak tree was down and gone forever! What had we done?

The Oak Tree's Message

The immediate answer to that question was something about saving time and making the roof installation easier to accomplish. This was not the same answer the neighboring old oak tree had to share. Actually, that old oak tree's method of communicating was best reflected in the phrase, "A picture is worth a thousand words." Almost within hours (or so it seemed) of removing the fallen tree, this neighboring old oak sent hundreds of acorns everywhere. The speed and volume of the acorns was shocking! The old oak tree pelted acorns against the house, hitting the windows with resounding gunshot-like sounds…so much so that I began to feel like I was under attack. This continued with such fervor that I was forced to stop my business-producing activities and go outside to confirm what I heard. The driveway was within inches of being totally covered with acorns! (At this rate, the driveway would be a different color within minutes.) Walking on this covering of round objects was indeed a challenge. Then there was the all-out attack of the acorns that were being projected at me. This barrage didn't stop that day. No, it went on *for over a week!* The old oak tree's visual message was one of anger, frustration, and refusal to accept the change that had been forced upon it.

Do you begin to see, how the old oak tree's message connects all of us to "being in nature and nature being in us"? Was the reaction of this old oak any different from our reactions when change is forced upon us? Don't we get angry and frustrated and sometimes refuse to accept change? Nature has marvelous messages to share with us if only we take the time to really listen, learn, and grow with the experience.

Take Time to Be Present

There's not a day that goes by that I forget to stop and look at the remaining old oak tree, feeling the same sense of loss that it feels for the fallen companion. The shade, the oxygen, the habitat, the food source…all that it gave…I was a part of that, too. I am that, I am…I am in nature, and nature is now in me. You are in nature, and nature is in you, if you take the time to be present.

So many parallels exist for that oak tree and me, *and you*. Although the oak tree was just one tree, its acorns are infinite. In a similar way, each of us only exist as a quantity of one, but our ideas are also infinite in number. The resulting trees from those acorns are exponential in numbers, as are the new possibilities from a human's ideas…and those new trees in nature and those new possibilities in us can reshape my life, *your life*, the lives of others, as well as the lives of future generations. Listen to the messages from an old oak tree, like "become all you are capable of becoming," "be your authentic self…be real" (regardless what other opinions of you and your worth might be), remember to "be in the now…be present," "take time to stop and smell the roses…to really listen, to learn, to grow with the experience," and like the oak tree…**"share your message with the world, for it will not fall on deaf ears."**

Perhaps Henry David Thoreau, American author, poet, and philosopher, said it best: "Though I do not believe that a plant will spring up where no seed has been, I have great faith in a seed. Convince me that you have a seed there, and I am prepared to expect wonders." Yes, that old oak tree's lasting message was to remind me that I am in nature and nature is in me (I am that, I am). The "seeds within us both" are capable of so much more than what is visible! Have faith and expect wonders!

Let the soul know the depth of its roots, the height of its branches where its dreams spread forth, and its strength to stand firm, always, with its inner knowing that in each of us is a message to share!

Beverly Ameykeller, a spiritual being having human experiences, lives life fully through the expressions of business owner, mentor, author, and edupreneur...the blend of educator with entrepreneur. With her background it's her nature to share what she learns to empower others along life's path, individually or to an audience. In addition to being a published author, Beverly further compliments life through creating family memories and music. Her first musical expression, Earthwaves, is releasing in 2008.

You can contact Beverly at www.BeverlyAmeykeller.com or 1-800-920-6906.

Manifest Success

Gratitude in the Midst of the Storm

How grateful are you for the storms raging through your life, the challenges you are facing, the uncertainty that arises when you least expect it? These are the very times you must have the most faith and be grateful.

It's the rough spots in my own life that I am most grateful for, because it was when life was coming at me with gale force winds and flooding rains that I had to depend on God the most. These times taught me to allow Him to show me my strengths. During these storms of life, I was stretched, pushed, pulled, and formed into who I am today.

As the Bible says: "The wise man builds his house upon the rock so that it will stand firm when the rain and wind beat upon the house. The foolish man builds his house upon the sand. Because the foolish man's house was not built on a firm foundation it fell when the wind and rain beat upon the house" (Matt. 7:24-27). I believe the Lord is our solid ground, and a life built on any other ground will crumble during a storm.

Thankful for the Storms

I am not saying I like the storms of life. Like everyone else, when things are not going well I sometimes become frustrated and uncomfortable. However, as I move through each challenge and the feelings that accompany it, by trusting in the Lord to show me the way, I find myself becoming stronger and more effective at living a positive life. So I have learned to be very thankful for these storms.

I believe that if there were no challenges in life, I would never have seen just how awesome God is. This requires me to be open and trusting in a higher power and to believe in myself.

God did not have to send these storms to show me his love, but I required the storms to see the love He has for me. God used these storms and challenges to show me how awesome a God he really is.

For instance, if I had not known individuals who lost their jobs, I would never have been able to see God as a provider. If I had not known people facing illness, I would have never seen the healing power of God. Each day miracles occur, and by being open to God, I am able to see them.

How do I have a grateful attitude in the midst of my storms? How do I share this with others so they can make it through their storms? I share with them the concept of expecting a storm to arrive as part of the plan.

You see, you are either in a storm right now, coming out of a storm, or a storm is about to hit. Either way, if you plan ahead, build a solid foundation and have faith, when the storm comes your house will continue to stand strong.

A Personal Example

About four years ago when my wife and I first were married, we shared with each other our beliefs and faith. We promised each other to make God the center of our marriage, as we both felt it was God who brought us together and God who would guide us along the path of staying together.

The first part of our marriage was wonderful. We never fought, we enjoyed each other, and we agreed on almost everything. Then the honeymoon stage ended, and we found ourselves in the middle of a very tough time. We walked through storm after storm as our faith, our trust in each other, and the very foundation of our marriage was being tested.

We found ourselves fighting about everything, large and small. We didn't agree on anything. Overall, it was a very draining experience for both of us, but neither of us ever lost our faith in God. After fighting, the smoke would clear and in the calm we would come together and talk about what had happened. We would say to each other, "I've been praying about what's happening, asking God to help us through this storm."

Sometimes I would lie awake at night, praying for God to give me the strength to stay and work things out. The storm we were in had a purpose; it was designed to test us and show us what our marriage was really built on. I feel that it was God's way of showing us how with Him as the center of our marriage together we could accomplish anything. There would never be a storm so great that we could not weather, as long as we stayed true to each other.

We learned to lean on each other, to trust in God, and to have faith. This is what brought us through the storm. I am happy to say that this storm has passed, and God has kept my wife and I together. We did our part by deciding not to give up when things were difficult.

Whether it is in work or family life, when things get tough, most people are tempted to walk away, and many do. But it is during these times that, if you are open to receiving, God will give you the wisdom and the courage to make it through and come out stronger, healthier, and more secure than ever before.

For my wife and me, this storm would have torn us apart and destroyed our marriage if we had not decided before the storm hit that we were going to build the house of our marriage on the foundation of God.

Building on Solid Ground

It doesn't matter if it is your business, your relationships, or your health – the key is building on solid ground. If you build on solid ground, you can weather any storm. Once the storm passes, you will find the blessings you were meant to receive.

Like most people, I would have liked an easier and less painful way to learn these life lessons. However, the easy road is not necessarily the best road, and the lessons learned through the easy road are not always the ones required to move forward into living a better and more fulfilling life. By moving through and reaching the other side of life's storms, growth occurs. For us, our marriage would not have grown to the level it has if it was not for the storms we weathered.

I expect there will be more storms ahead, but because God showed Himself to us during this last storm and we have faith in Him as an unchanging God, we know without a doubt that He will always be there for us.

In reality, the pain, uncertainty and fear faced during a storm is the pain of growth and change. If we thank God when life is good and everything is going our way, it will be easier to remember God's presence when life is rough and we feel like we are drowning in the flood of life's storms. When we have a strong belief in God, we are never truly alone.

Ryan Bradley lives in the "City by the Bay" with his best friend and soul mate Jessica. His company is based on the motto "find the need, fill the need." Each of the innovative and solutions-oriented products Ryan promotes has a specific purpose and passion that drives that product to excellence by answering the question, "How may we serve?" Feel free to contact him at 1-888-304-3880

Debbi Chambers

All with One
One with All

"Starboard side!" I heard over the roar of the boat motor as I lay, belly down, on the bow of the speeding boat. As I reached my open palm into the warm gulf water, a jolt of energy rushed up my arm. There it was again, the smooth, cool skin of a dolphin. One after another, as if they were waiting in queue, dolphins surfed close enough to receive a loving stroke on their back, a human touch – *my* touch.

The day had been spent with our private dive master, diving and frolicking with a variety of underwater friends. Most notable was the nursery of baby seals, under the watchful eyes of their mothers, on a tiny island off the Mexican coast. The resemblance of these fun-loving creatures to our family pets was remarkable. As the babies would gently bite and shake our flippers, the adults would glide by our masks, making eye contact, as if peeking inside to see if they recognized their underwater guests.

As we made our way to dock, the fabulous multicolor sunset took my breath away, and I had that recurring knowing, *I AM one with everything, everyone, under our heavens.*

"All things are connected like the blood that unites us all. Man did not weave the web of life; he is merely a strand in it. Whatever he does to the web, he does to himself." ~ Chief Seattle, as translated by Ted Perry

We Are All Connected

Imagine a world where everyone not only understood the significance of this but reflected it in their every thought, feeling, word, and action. We are all born with this innate knowing, this sense of oneness planted deep within us. And while we are individually the center and creator of our own physical world (our own chosen reality), spiritually and at a cellular level we are all connected. Each of us is an integral part of the greater universe in which we live and create together. Our completeness depends on one another. All that we think, feel, and do, will be, in some way, at some place and time, collectively realized. As we strengthen ourselves, we strengthen each other. What we reinforce in others, we reinforce in ourselves. Recognition of this great ability, and even greater responsibility, empowers us to embrace our infinite potential, not only as individual human beings but also as a part of all humanity.

The awareness of this oneness and connection with everyone and everything is vital to your success as you run a business. As you create your business, you create an extension of yourself and a piece of the world. As you manage your business, you manage yourself and the universe. To serve yourself, you must serve others, because when you serve others, you ARE serving yourself.

It is only with the intention of more life to all and less to none that true success can be found. We each hold the ability to change the world – one thought, one action, one person, one cell at a time. Like ripples in a pond, everything we do creates a movement in the water and a momentum that affects the next ripple and the next ripples after that. The more attention we give to this throughout our everyday activities, the better our ability will be to multiply our efforts exponentially until, one day, all of our efforts come together to form a giant wave of success.

Passion Is the Fuel

How do you best utilize your individual efforts to ripple the waters of the world? How do you keep that momentum moving into a wave of success? PASSION! Passion is found where your desires for others are equal to your desires for yourself. The embodiment of "love your neighbor as you love yourself," passion ignites you to create a better world for all. Passion fuels you throughout the journey. It is passion that you feel when you embrace your connection to and oneness with all. It is passion that leads to the most fulfilling and least resistant path to success. Your path to success lies within all that you do with passion.

No matter what your chosen field, your success will be measured by the value you provide to others. Realize, however, that in order to *give* value you must first *have* value. Value yourself above all else so that you will be able to give value to others. You must love yourself to give love. This kind of giving can't be done graciously when you are waiting for the love you are giving to be returned, because then you are giving out of the hope for reciprocation. If you unconditionally love yourself first, you can give without attachment, confident that you are deserving and already receiving all that you desire, with complete gratitude for already having it. This is the realization of your oneness and connection to each and every being. Loving your neighbor as yourself means loving yourself first and loving yourself – a lot!

More to All and Less to None

As you provide more to all and less to none, you can rest assured that you too are a part of the all. Look at every idea, product, or service that you have to offer and ask, "How can I provide greater service to more individuals? How can I add value to more lives with this product? How will all of this give more value to me?" The answers to these questions will always lead you to greater success.

Your connection to everyone and everything is infinite. There are no boundaries, no exceptions, and no limits. Every thought, every feeling, and every action you take has an effect on someone, something, somewhere. To this end, the least resistant path to success is one where you keep your thoughts, feelings, and actions aligned with your passion and your desire to serve and to love others just as you love yourself. Your thoughts inspire your feelings, and you are propelled into action. When all three (thoughts, feelings, and actions) are in agreement and in alignment, you experience an integrity that leads to inevitable success.

Imagine how seamlessly success would occur in your business if you thought only of how to serve others more, if you were endlessly passionate, and if every action was the direct result of this. Imagine how seamlessly success would come to you if you valued yourself enough to share yourself with others. This creates an unstoppable business. It never tires, it never fades, and it never dulls. It is true and complete in its integrity. This creates a business that changes the world.

With the intention of adding more life to all and less to none, we create the first ripples in the water that will lead to a wave of success – not only for ourselves but for all. The passion in our hearts fuels the momentum for an endless and effortless journey, while the integrity of our minds and the trueness of our actions multiply our efforts exponentially. Above all else, though, it is the recognition of our oneness with each other and our connection to all of life that provides us with the powerful foundation on which to build a fulfilling and purposeful life.

"Infinite Peaceful Possibilities"

Debbi Chambers is the creator of the award receiving "Manifesting Garden-Create Your Garden of Infinite Possibilities, A 45 Day Goal Achievement Adventure (www.faith-creations.com). Together with her 'Web Success Diva', Maria Reyes-McDavis, she created Network Marketing Success 2.0 System, a revolutionary, cutting edge Internet lead and client generator.

Visit www.networkmarketing20system.com to receive a free viral marketing instructional video.

Manifest Success

Joan Maresh-Hansen

A Series of
Serendipitous Events

When "in the flow" – know you're on the right path.

My life has been a series of serendipitous experiences. Again and again, I have seen amazing things fall effortlessly into place, and through them all has run one common thread: a strong belief that my desire would come to be. I have always believed that ideas are God talking inside our heads – when we get an idea, we must trust that the ways and means to make our ideas a reality *will* present themselves, and when they do, we must step into action. Inspired actions are the key to results!

A powerful energy is unleashed when a person feels inspired. As Patanjali said over twenty centuries ago, "Dormant forces, faculties, and talents come alive, and you discover yourself to be a greater person by far than you ever dreamed yourself to be." If you have ever felt inspired by a purpose or a calling, then you know the feeling of Spirit working through you. I certainly have, as the following story will show. Pay particular attention to the effortless ways each of the events transpired.

My incredible teaching life spanned thirty-four amazing years spent with very talented young people. My students were featured in national magazines, had their art in state-adopted textbooks, and always made me look good at state and national conferences. As an art educator, I worked to bring positive change into my students' lives. In the 1980s I got a wake up call when I realized that my students would not be prepared for the workforce of the future unless they had some mastery of technology. Brilliant as they were, they were also technologically illiterate!

This was long before computers were routinely placed in schools. Back then, I did not own a computer myself, had no access to one, and knew nothing of hardware, software, or their inherent possibilities. Still, I had a vision for a computer lab on the school grounds where students could get the education and training in technology they so sorely required. I became obsessed with my goal, and for thirteen years I wrote grant after grant, searching for the funds to bring my dream to life.

Eventually inspiration arrived: I decided to host an event at my school to demonstrate the new evolving technologies opening up in the workforce and world. A computer lab would be set up and manned with instructors to teach art and design applications and speakers who would address all the exciting new possibilities. The event would be called "A Day in Cyberspace."

That same year, the National Art Education (NAEA) conference was scheduled to come to Houston. NAEA brings approximately 3,000 members from all over the nation to the host city. Perusing the NAEA newsletter, it occurred to me to call the man coordinating this huge event and tell him about "A Day in Cyberspace." I tracked down the number and made the call. "Hello, you don't know me. I am from Sugar Land, Texas, and I want to talk to you about technology at the Houston conference." After listening to my idea, he said, "I just opened the Houston conference folder on technology and…there's nothing in it." After a moment of silence, reflecting on what just happened, we both burst out laughing. He gave me the name of the person presiding over the Houston technology committee. It turned out to be a colleague of mine – the art coordinator for a nearby school district. I called her the next evening.

We spoke during a break in an educational seminar I was attending, and I told her about my ideas. Her reply stunned me: "Joan, I have not had a moment to work on this and do not see things getting any better.

Would you head this committee?" I swallowed and said, "Well, yes!" After hanging up, a mixture of fear and uncertainty threatened to overwhelm me until I remembered where I was – that evening's educational seminar was at Houston's Apple headquarters!

I walked back into the meeting room where an Apple executive, also a friend, was standing. As I relayed to him what had just happened, that first flash of trepidation shifted to excitement over this incredible opportunity for 3,000 educators to be shown what could be done with technology in the hands of creative people. I said, "Do you realize the potential impact on these teachers and, more importantly, on their students?" He smiled. "How many computers do you foresee in your event?" I said I had envisioned three labs of twenty computers each, with workshops going simultaneously from morning till night.

Others listening asked if they could assist, and in the first few moments of being the committee chair, participants were volunteering, equipment was being located, and the speakers who were presenting that night were both offering to present and suggesting other people they could contact to speak about the other software applications being used in the art industry.

Within a few days, the Apple executive contacted me and said a local school district had ordered sixty computers (yes, the exact number!) that were scheduled to arrive days before the conference. He said he could have them delivered to the conference site where his team would load the software required by the presenters, clean off the machines afterwards, and deliver them back to the school district that had consented to the idea. Another company offered to loan us projectors free of charge for each presenter.

It gets better. I was asked to oversee the scheduling of the technology presenters for the labs. That meant that all the presenters contacted me, which allowed me to communicate updates and requests to everyone involved in this dream-come-true event. In another synchronicity, one slot for a keynote address in a super session was vacant. I informed the committee that a new acquaintance of mine, Los Angeles resident and educational guru David Thornburg, was speaking at another Texas conference and was willing to step in at a greatly reduced rate. They accepted his offer.

Very close to the time of the conference, the executive director of NAEA asked me, in a somewhat irritated tone, how I planned to insure these sixty machines. It came to me out of the blue to request that the equipment be placed under the umbrella of the NAEA conference's insurance. This man was known to be a little intimidating, but I can remember the shift in his tone and manner as I excitedly shared with him my vision for this opportunity to change lives. He softened and said, "I will have to call you back." Ten minutes later came the news, "It's done!"

NAEA conference labs were set up and tickets sold out prior to the conference. It all went so smoothly that it could only have been what I now understand as "in the flow."

All the presenters, all the hardware, all the software, the several committees formed to set up and take down the labs – assistance came from all directions with almost no effort. Leaders and team members of the executive council visited the labs numerous times and commented favorably on the success of its implementation. This event changed the history of the association as well as the lives of many people, including mine.

The next year, I was honored at the state association conference as Texas's Secondary Art Educator of the Year. The following spring, I was sent to San Francisco for ten days, all expenses paid, to receive NAEA's prestigious National Art Educator of the Year award. After stepping down off the stage, a gentleman said to me, "You are the one!" He asked me to start the communication graphics program at G.W. Carver High School, a Houston art magnet school. I agreed, but only if it was to be a Mac lab. His answer? "It will be a *dream* Mac Lab." And it was!

At Carver, my students and I created the first electronic media program in the state of Texas, only the third in the country. We had visitors from all over the state and the nation. We collaborated on a McGraw Hill/Glencoe book, *Digital Studio Projects*, were featured in eighteen national *School Arts* magazine articles, and won third place in Xerox's "Strut Your Stuff" competition. The amazing thing about this contest is that we were the only high school entry; the first, second, fourth, and fifth place winners were huge graphic design companies. How true are the words of Samuel Johnson: "Our aspirations are our possibilities"!

Joan Maresh-Hansen is a lifelong educator, contributing editor in numerous books and magazine features, and frequent speaker at the state and national level. Her passions mix art and technology in online virtual classrooms, creating connections between educators across the world. Visit her Web sites for exemplary evidence of her rich teaching life and to access monthly bonuses. To learn of her life in and beyond the public classroom, visit:

http://www.artworkontheweb.com
http://www.evesgardentexas.com
http://www.reachingnewrealities.com
http://www.coolclickchicks.com

Manifest Success

Jeffery Combs

Emotional Resilience

As an entrepreneur, emotional resilience allows you not to take situations personally. When someone criticizes you or gives you input, instead of coming from a position where you have to defend yourself, it's often better to agree and see the other person's perspective. Understanding where the person is coming from is so much more important than being confrontational. Two fools arguing are two fools arguing.

Instead of arguing at this point in my journey, I now come from the position, "You be right, I'll be rich." I no longer have to be right. I used to spend much of my time overreacting and proving myself right. I was coming from a place in my consciousness that told me I wasn't good enough, so I felt that I had to prove that I was loveable.

Most of us are conditioned that love is something we have to earn. As small children, we have to perform to receive love. When you can come from a place of unconditional love within your heart, that's when you begin to attract it to your reality. That's when you have love for other people, love for the game, love for life, love for the journey. That's when you start to radiate and telepathically send thought waves into the Universe that say, "I am a magnet for love. I am a magnet for peace. I am a magnet for prosperity. I am a magnet for assisting people. I am a leader." It is very powerful to resonate from this position of emotional resilience.

Words Create Reality

Let's examine your feelings about a variety of words associated with adversity. Emotional resilience is the key: how you feel about the present adversity, how you feel about what's happening in the moment, and how you feel about the present situation. (Note that I didn't say, "How you *think* about it," because when most people think, they start to overthink. They start to analyze.)

How about the term *devastating?* Have you ever been devastated by a situation? Is that really true? Were you devastated, or was it just a challenge? Words that allow you to deal with devastation are overcoming, letting go, releasing, and changing your perception.

Another term is *victim.* The opposite of victim is victor. Many people operate from a victim mentality. That way, they can blame everyone, everything, and every situation except the real person who is responsible. Instead of being the victim, ask yourself, "How did I attract this to my reality? What will I gain because of this? How can I stop being a victim?" At this point, you start to develop character.

Let's take a look at the term *surviving.* Your objective is not to just survive. Your objective is to flourish. If you are in a survival mode, ask yourself, "How did I learn to operate like this?" Did your parents teach you that struggle is noble? Were you taught lack and scarcity? Surviving isn't flourishing. Flourishing is prosperity, flow, radiating, producing, and attracting. When you flourish, situations find you rather than you struggling to find them.

How about the phrase "the events that shape your life"? Average people let events shape their lives. Their mindset is, "Because I grew up over here, I can't ever become that." "Because I don't have a college education, I feel less than." "Because I failed at three business ventures before, I can't afford to take another risk."

42

From Chaos to Flow

Getting overwhelmed or creating chaos (or attracting chaos) is another adverse situation that many people experience. They live cluttered lives. They live in cluttered houses. They work in cluttered offices. They are overwhelmed by chaos. Have you ever gotten into someone's car, and there were empty bags from fast-food restaurants, tapes, and books all over the seat, the floor, the floor mat? This is usually an indication of chaos in their lives. If that is you, here's the question: *What are you going to do about the chaos?* Now, I'm not suggesting that you have to be a perfectionist, but how much energy does chaos drain from your life? The opposite of chaos is flow. Create a routine. Let go of some of the chaos. Ask yourself, "How much clutter can I release?"

I have coached many, many people who have offices or homes that are an absolute mess. They have stacks and stacks of boxes and magazines. Have you ever seen this type of person's garage when you pass by in the street? There's so much stuff in the garage that they can't even park their cars in it. This usually reflects the chaos that's in someone's mind as well. Imagine what it would be like to operate without all this chaos. Imagine what it would be like to operate in the hands-free zone. Imagine what it would be like to operate from flow, where life is fun and easy and clutter-free.

Someone who has a lot of chaos usually has challenges with letting go. They hold on to everything – not only their clutter, but also their emotions and their past – so they can keep themselves in chaos. Would success contradict your struggle? Would letting go of all this chaos allow you to be free? If you were free, would you no longer be able to struggle? How would that feel? Ask yourself right now, "What clutter will I release from my life?" "If I released the clutter, would chaos no longer serve me?" "How does being overwhelmed take me out of the game?"

The Fear of Success

Many people actually overcommit to too many tasks so they can truly never commit to any of them. I've seen so many people attempt to do three or four entrepreneurial endeavors at one time and then say, "I'm creating multiple streams of income." When someone makes that statement, they're usually not making any money in any of their four ventures. There's nothing wrong with having multiple streams of income, but it's best to master one business first. So many people do this unconsciously, as a method of self-sabotage, so they can never actually succeed. These people set themselves up to fail, knowing that if they take on more than they can handle, they will never succeed. This is called the fear of success.

Ask yourself, "What can I actually let go of in my life? What will I remove from my life, my garage, my office, and my file cabinet?" When you do this, you start to create space in the Universe for more flow to come in. When you have all the doors blocked, it's hard for prosperity, abundance, and the right people to find you, because the message you are sending telepathically is, "I am a chaos addict; I am attracted to the drama; I am attracted to the struggle." The opposite of this is, "Struggle-aholic no more: I am dropping the drama." What drama are you willing to drop? What chaos are you willing to release yourself from?

Many people resist change, because change represents death – not death on the physical plane, but the death of an era. That's why so many people hold on to their past. There is no growth or reward without risk, and this requires facing adverse situations. You're going to have to handle challenges in the moment, and sometimes you'll have to change how you've been changing.

Breakthroughs

Sometimes you change, and you don't even know you've changed. This is when the your internal communication has changed, and the compounded effects start to take place. This is when you really become the leader people are looking for, with that belief, that sense of certainty, that strong conviction, that strong will. It's very important to develop a heartfelt vision – a reason to succeed, a reason to overcome, a reason to prevail, and a reason to handle adversity and break through the walls of your own consciousness. A breakthrough is when you see an obstacle and say, "I will not be denied. This will not overtake me, it will not overcome me – I will live my dreams, I will become the person that I deserve to be."

Only when your pain becomes great enough will you change. You might live your life to minimize short-term pain, but it's the incorrect beliefs that drive you and cause you pain today. Why do you live with it? Because the pain of change is greater and this is typically why you don't change. Many people will contradict themselves so they don't have to fully commit to the process. They say, "I hope, I wish, I tried, I'd like to, if only...."

Live from Your Heart

There is no such thing as luck. You have to be able to go where no man has gone. You have to be able to make the breakthroughs. You have to feel in your heart. You have to know. You have to trust. You have to believe. You have to see. You have to have a heartfelt centered vision of where you're going, what you're becoming, what you'll do. When you can operate from a sense of passion, you're radiating from your heart. You're sending this message, "Become a part of what I'm doing," and that, my friends, is when people want to be a part of what you are creating – because you are emotionally resilient; you are coming from you heart, not your head.

Jeffery Combs is an internationally recognized trainer in the network marketing & direct sales industry. Jeff specializes in prospecting, leadership, personal breakthroughs, prosperity consciousness, scripts, mindset training, and all levels of effective marketing. His many audio training programs benefit entrepreneurs & direct sales people at all levels of conscious development. He has personally consulted with 1000's of clients as a personal coach and mentor, and is highly sought after by entrepreneurs, direct sales people, network marketers, and people from all walks of life. Jeff is the President of Golden Mastermind Seminars Inc., and is committed to assisting people change the way they feel in order to achieve their goals and dreams!

Jeff is available to you and your company for coaching and speaking, and has developed a special package of training materials and professional guidance that will assist you and your team to create maximum results now! For further information, please call 800-595-6632 or visit his web site at www.goldenmastermind.com.

Total Health and the Mind-Body Connection

In my twenties I developed a passion for fitness and health, and I can't think of a better passion. I have gone from being a skinny, 150-pound, unhealthy young man with a negative self-image, to a completely healthy and fit 200-pound, lean, muscular fifty-four-year-old. I have a totally positive self-image and the body of a man in his early thirties. On this journey, I have developed a lifestyle that has created a very healthy body and strong mind.

Total health is when every part of your body works together optimally – when your mind and body are one and, through your lifestyle and mindset, you provide your body with everything it requires to live a fulfilling, stress-free, disease-free, happy, and long life. It is a four-sided lifestyle, focusing first on the mind-body connection (self-help) and then on nutrition, exercise (aerobic and anaerobic), and supplementation (vitamins and minerals). The key is learning the science behind these aspects and tying them together into one common sense program that will become a way of life. This will enable you to reach optimal health, fight disease, and reverse aging.

Your Most Important Muscle

Why do many people start a health program and fail? They fail because they do not train the most powerful muscle in their body – their mind. It's their mind that fails, not their body. Anthony Robbins believes that 80 percent of success in life is psychology (the mind) and 20 percent is mechanics (the body). Developing the mind-body connection is essential in achieving success in your life. We all have a mind-body connection, but many of us have no control over it, and so, subconsciously or unknowingly, we use it in mostly negative ways. Robbins states that what we *actually* do and what we *can* do are two different things. What we *actually* do is usually far less than what we *can* do. We choose not to live up to our potential.

If you haven't programmed or exercised your mind, then any attempt to become healthy will probably fail. You shape yourself by how you use your mind. First, you must know what you want. Most people get caught up in their day-to-day activities. They are reactive rather than proactive. They react to events instead of purposefully planning how their day will go. They do not prioritize or take the time to look at the big picture. People don't plan to fail; they fail to plan.

I believe there are two kinds of people – those who simply exist, and those who create their own destiny. There are leaders and followers. Do you know which one you are? Leaders have goals and a plan of action. They know their strengths and weaknesses, and they are always working on strengthening the latter. Followers never get in touch with their inner selves; they don't have a game plan or any direction in the game of life.

Observe Your Thoughts and Self-Talk

How do you get in touch with your mind-body connection? You start by observing and becoming aware of your thoughts on an ongoing basis. Notice *what* you think about and *how* you think. What topics do you tend to dwell upon? Which ones do you not dwell upon? Which ones do you avoid thinking about? Are the topics in the future or mainly in the past? How much of your thinking is positive and how much is negative? Is your thinking in mostly mental images or self-talk? Self-talk is the constant chatter that goes on inside your head. Is it critical or supportive? Is it angry or calm? You must familiarize yourself with your ways of thinking and your thinking patterns. If you aren't aware of how you think, then you won't be able to change your thoughts so that the feelings they produce are more to your liking. By managing your thoughts, you'll directly influence your emotions.

How do you talk to yourself? Do you constantly criticize yourself or others mentally? Do you complain about your life, your faults, or how unfair life is? Do you tell yourself that you're going to fail at something? What if you had a friend who hung out with you every day and made only negative comments – how would you feel? Negative self-talk is debilitating. If you tell yourself you can't do something, then you won't be able to do it. It's a self-fulfilling prophecy. You may be so used to doing this that you don't consciously pay attention to it. By daily observation, you will discover your negative self-talk patterns – they have become habits formed by time and repetition. Any habit you have, whether good or bad, is formed by repetition.

Recondition Your Habits

When you recognize negative self-talk, remind yourself that it's an old habit you are going to change. Reassure and calm yourself. Remind yourself to remain confident, positive, and focused on the future. There is enough negativity in your environment to deal with and cope with without sabotaging yourself.

Old habits aren't broken immediately. We've all heard the cliché, "Old habits are hard to break." It's true. You must repeat the process time after time until your positive and uplifting thoughts have become new habits. And it's not that anxiety, stress, or depressed feelings won't emerge at times. Life comes with its share of ups and downs, but it's how you deal with the "downs" that truly makes you who you are.

You must be able to manage your emotional state. You're in control, and you must use that ability. What controls your emotional state is what you focus on. YOU make the decisions about what your mind focuses on. How do you control the focus? You do it by asking yourself the right questions. Instead of asking, "Why am I so fat?" and getting depressed, ask, "What could I do to become healthy?" Turn the question into a positive, motivating one. Condition yourself to feel differently about the concepts of pain and pleasure and the associations you make. You must recondition the way you think – your feelings, associations, and beliefs. You developed these ways of thinking over the course of time. They have been formed as a result of experience and environment. These feelings, associations, and beliefs are what limit you.

Control Your Stress and Lighten Up

It is a well-known fact that stress creates and multiplies physical health problems. You can program your mind to deal with stress. The first step is realizing when you are stressed. You must learn not to let stress control you. Dealing with it by smoking, drinking, overeating, using drugs, or simply shutting down is harmful to your health – they merely postpone the issues. Identify the things you can and cannot control. Don't stress about things that are out of your control, those things you cannot change. My advice is to avoid taking life too seriously. Lighten up a little. Everything is not a crisis. Always keep things in perspective, to the best of your ability.

Success at anything requires goal-setting and action. When you focus on your goals and take action on a daily basis, you will achieve them. The alternative is to wander aimlessly through life, taking whatever it throws at you. Build one day at a time until your actions become habits. All successful people have great discipline and take consistent action. Successful people have mentors and build a team around themselves. A saying I recently heard is, "You are the sum of your best five friends." Surround yourself with focused, positive people!

Discovering the mind-body connection will transform your body and your health. Remember, your mind must be in shape before your body.

The body follows the mind. You've got to believe. *You can do it!* The mind-body connection impacts every phase of your life: health, business, relationships, and so on. Take control of your life – realize that you get out of life what you put into it. Live long, live healthy, and stop the hands of time!

Rico Connor is a fifty-four-year-old self-taught health and fitness expert, author, champion bodybuilder, and business entrepreneur. He is a regular expert contributor in the field of mind-body connection, nutrition, strength training, and supplementation for two national magazines. His book, *Total Health for Life, Mind & Body: The Baby Boomer's Bible of Health,* is available on Amazon.com. Rico teaches individuals how to achieve optimal health, fight disease, and reverse aging – as well as train the mind for success, happiness, and fulfillment. Visit: **www.totalhealth4life. net** to receive his free monthly newsletter and notification of future offers. As a special gift, you will also receive free the first chapter of his highly acclaimed book.

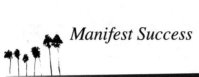

Manifest Success

Judy G Cook

One Chapter at a Time
Our Lives are Like Chapters of a Book

Have you ever tumbled out of bed and felt as if the floor opened and you fell into a bottomless pit? If this is your story…stop! I found a way out, and you can too.

I was born in Atlanta, Georgia into an average income family. When I was born my dad said, "Send her back. I only want boys."

I became "daddy's little girl." Dad took me fishing, hunting, and camping. Mom thought I should learn to be a girl, so she sent me to modeling school, but in order to have the approval of both parents, I only agreed to model hunting clothes.

Trying to please everyone, I was like a rubber duck floating on the ocean, being washed in and out by the tide. I never tried to chart my own course or take charge of my own life.

All my girlfriends loved my dad, and I wanted to be just like him with his fun-loving personality.

My parents divorced when I was fifteen years old, and I went to live with my father. I graduated from high school in 1968 and moved to New York to work.

I met a professional golfer, several years my senior, and we were married in 1972. We divorced in 1979, because I was looking for a "father figure" to take care of me.

What I didn't realize then was that by letting someone else think for you, you are making a choice...the choice for someone else to dictate your life. Life is all about choices, and if you aren't making them, then you aren't living.

After my divorce, I met my "one true love" boyfriend, who loved to party. Our first year together was good, just one big party that later turned into a sick relationship. He stalked me, beat me, and would then bring me flowers. I had always loved life, but I started hating it. I felt like a plastic doll...if you cut me open I would be empty inside.

"Whacko Ben" moved on, and I continued to party. I never had "enough." I always wanted more, and I would buy things I didn't even want just trying to fill up the empty hole inside of me.

One weekend I was so drunk that my friends took my keys to keep me from driving, not knowing I had an extra set that I kept hidden in the car.

I drove down the road as fast as I could, taking a sharp curve; instead of hitting the brakes, I hit the gas and went flying off the road. I flipped three times, hit a palm tree, and was trapped upside down in my car, which was crushed flat. The paramedics had to cut me out, and I was taken to the hospital, where I woke up the next morning. I didn't remember leaving the party, the accident, or anything.

The doctors told me that I was the luckiest person alive, because no one seeing the car believed that I could have survived. I stayed in the hospital two days with a brace on my neck. But the question I kept asking myself was, *Why* did *I survive?*

After deciding I must be living in the wrong state, I left Florida and moved back home to Atlanta, Georgia to live with my mother and her new husband, who tried to teach me to manage my finances. I got a good job and started saving money.

When I moved back home I was broken, both mentally and physically. Yet the better my life seemed on the outside, the emptier I felt inside. I went back to my old lifestyle of hanging out at bars. My mother wanted to get me into a twelve-step program, but I wasn't ready.

On the 4th of July weekend in 1985, I had a friend over. We were getting ready for a big party. We were dancing around my apartment having a great time. I danced into the kitchen and the next thing I knew, I was lying flat on the kitchen floor. I must have tripped over something, but I was going into convulsions and turning blue. My friend drove me to the nearest hospital, but I had to admit myself because he knew my mother didn't want me dating him, and if I died he was afraid of being accused of murder.

I tried filling out the papers but couldn't. My family doctor happened to be in the hospital, and he sent the police to get my mother, who got there before they shaved my head and took me into surgery because I had a blood clot on my brain. My heart stopped beating during surgery, but they were able to bring me back. I remember waking up the next morning, all bandaged and screaming because my head hurt so much.

My mom sat next to my bed, and I could see the disappointed look in her eyes, looking at a daughter who just couldn't seem to get her act together.

I developed more blood clots on the brain, and during a second surgery they lost my heartbeat again. After the surgery, the doctors told my mother that even though I had survived, I might be like a three-year-old, or in a wheelchair. I stayed in intensive care for the next two weeks.

The depression was terrible – the doctors called it "post accident syndrome" and told me I would work though it in a few weeks. I was at an all-time low, and I coped with it the only way I knew how, with pills and alcohol.

I had to have a small plate put in my head, and afterwards I had problems coming out of the anesthesia. Everyone said I was lucky to have survived. I didn't feel lucky. Why *had* I survived?

After my partying had gotten so bad, even my party friends were backing off; my mother finally got me into that twelve-step program. I lasted ninety days, and I was so happy I had made it that long that I bought a case of beer and went out to the lake to celebrate.

My Wake-Up Call

September 13, 1986 is a day I will never forget. A turning point in my life, it was the day my mother had a heart attack and died, and it was the day I woke up.

I realized that I was thirty-six years old and couldn't take care of myself. My mother had been my safety net from all of life's trials and tribulations. Sitting on the bathroom floor, I burned a candle and begged God to take me out of my misery because I couldn't live without my mother.

Finally, I went back to work, and a lady I worked with kept begging me to join her in a twelve-step program to overcome my addictions. I knew I couldn't continue on the road I was taking. I had come to a crossroads: it was either get assistance or die.

Today I love my life! In 1997, I backpacked around the world. I am writing a book about my life. I have a good job assisting people with weight loss, a beautiful home, and a Harley-Davidson motorcycle that I love riding in events to raise money for charities. I am indeed a free spirit. I am no longer nor will I ever be again the "Addiction Diva."

You can empower yourself by identifying your goals and working towards them. Life is like a book – you have to live it one chapter at a time.

You must forgive yourself for past mistakes and not beat yourself up over yesterday. Today I counsel young women about abuse, alcoholism, drugs, and low self-esteem. It is never too late in life to heal and make a change. The greatest joy you can have is giving to others and assisting them.

"God began doing a good work in you, and I am sure He will continue it until it is finished." (Philippians 1:16).

"I can do all things through Christ who strengthens me." (Philippians 4: 3)

Judy G. Cook lives in Atlanta, Georgia where she presently works with men and women in weight loss management. With over twenty-two years of experience in all types of addition areas, her focus is making the world a better place. She attended Bauder Fashion College and enjoys enhancing other women's lives. She is currently writing her life story and can be contacted at cookharley@yahoo.com. Judy's motto is "Become All You Can Be!"

Scott Davenport

Living Life
with Eyes Wide Open
Taking Advantage of the Opportunities You See

Seeing opportunities and taking advantage of them is one of the keys to success in life. Opportunities are there for everyone, but most people convince themselves it's too hard or too much work or the breaks are always for someone else. My example of this began back in the mid-eighties. I had just graduated from college with a business degree. I didn't have the slightest idea of how to use it. Most of my friends moved to Atlanta and entered the bottom rung of the corporate ladder. (For some reason this did not appeal to me in the least, and now I know why.)

A few weeks into my task of finding myself, one of my fraternity brothers called from Chicago, where his father had set him up with an apartment downtown and an entry-level position on the trading floor. He asked me to come for a visit, check out the city and the trading floor. So, with nothing better to do, I packed my suitcases and flew up for a visit. What should have been a short trip turned into a three week adventure, and I got five job offers to boot. The trading floor was the most alive place I'd ever been, and it gave me goose bumps just thinking about going to work every day. I flew back just long enough to get my things out of storage and break the news to my parents, and back to the city I went.

Things moved fast on the trading floor. Within a few months, I had bounced around from firm to firm, always jockeying for a better position, as if I myself was being traded as a commodity myself. I soaked up every shred of information about how things worked. Traders are always on the lookout for moldable young talent who can handle the pressure and are serious about learning the business. I worked for a small firm, a big firm, a local trader, and then a proprietary trading group that at one time traded 35 percent of the volume in the Deustche Mark and Japanese Yen option pits. I had never seen a place that got so much done so efficiently in such a small time frame. It seemed that the faster trading went, the more focused everybody got. I loved it! This was where I was supposed to be, yet I never would have discovered it if I hadn't jumped outside the box and taken a chance.

Solving Challenges

Problem solving is an exercise that nobody likes yet everyone has to do in life. People have different ways of dealing with problem situations. Some people simply run away or push their problems aside to deal with later. Some people face their problems head-on and are always ready for the next thing. The fact is that if you are afraid to try something new, you'll never give yourself a chance to pass or fail. The success you receive when you surpass an obstacle will give you the confidence to take on more and more. The first step is always the hardest.

I'm the kind of guy who likes to get things done and not worry about who gets the credit. I think it's such a waste of time and energy to rush to get something done in a hurry, only to find you have to go back and do the whole project over again. There is less chance of making a costly mistake by taking the time to analyze the procedures and by following a logical progression.

Defining Moment

Just the other day, my fourteen-year-old son came to me and said that he needed to talk. As parents know, this can be a loaded statement. He went on to tell me that he had fallen behind in his algebra class, and he was worried about his grade. I asked him how this could have happened if he listening in class, doing the homework, and studying for tests? He said that he had missed handing in some homework, he had not corrected his in-class worksheets, and he didn't know how to work some of the problems on the last test. He winced, thinking he knew what was coming. I thought about the situation for a moment and then said, "I understand." He said, "What?" in disbelief. I told him that I understood how easy it is to get sidetracked in life and lose focus, or get so overwhelmed with what seems like everything coming at us at once that we can't handle things as we normally would. I explained to him that the next step he takes would define him as a person and would be a strong measure of his character. "Will you shrug your shoulders and profess that everyone is against you, or will you say, 'I have to fix this'?" I asked him. He replied, "I have to fix this." He went on to tell me how he planned to get back on the right track. Needless to say, I was very pleased. Then it occurred to me that if we hadn't had this little conversation, he might not have known how to handle this situation, and it could have just gotten worse.

All of our experiences – good, bad, or indifferent – make us who we are today and affect how we relate to others. We have the power to decide how we will handle any situation and to decipher how the consequences or rewards will affect us, as well as those around us.

Scott Davenport is a CTA with over twenty-two years of experience as a futures and options strategist. Before joining the OIO team in 1992, he was a company risk analyst for a large commodity trading firm in Chicago. Scott also worked on the both the floor of the Chicago Mercantile Exchange and the Chicago Board of Trade, where he was accepted for membership. Scott invites you to call him anytime to discuss your investment and financial goals. You can reach him at 888-562-0568 or scottdav@oio.com.

Manifest Success

Patrick Dougher

Discovering My Internal Gift Changed My Life...Forever

"Mr. Dougher, do you realize that 99 percent of all the freshmen enrolled are placed above you? Are you sure you wouldn't rather go to a junior college to make sure that college is your cup of tea?"

Ouch! That hurt.

I knew I was not the smartest kid on the block, but the eloquent words my college academic advisor used to paint a bleak picture of my potential success at Texas A&M cut me deeply; I had never been called an idiot so proficiently in my whole life.

I had to work much harder than my classmates in high school to get Bs and Cs. My SAT scores barely met the minimum requirements for admission to Texas A&M. My interest in geology and my dad's desire to steer me toward a lucrative career had led selecting petroleum engineering as my major.

Shortly before setting foot on campus for orientation, I discovered that petroleum engineering required more math than I wanted. In order to change my major to geology, my very first stop after arriving on campus was the office of my academic advisor.

Never Quit!

As I sat in his office with his words ringing in my ears, I realized I had two choices. I could give in and select a different college, or I could draw upon the same determination, persistence, and love of learning that had brought me this far. At that moment, I made myself two promises: "I will never quit," and "I will never be called an idiot again."

During the next five years, I worked harder than I ever had before. I did not give up. After graduation, when geologists were being laid off daily, I accepted a position in communication sales. This turned out to be one of the greatest turning points in my life.

In 1999, I was invited to attend an introductory self-improvement workshop called The Road Adventure in Richardson, Texas. The program, a multi-weekend seminar, is like Dr. Phil on steroids. I was so intrigued by what I learned in Part 1 that I attended all four parts over the next few months.

One of the drills of Part 3 was a brief seven-question test to identify my primary internal gift. The test indicated that my primary internal gift was teaching. It did not seem possible that such a simple test could be accurate or that I could possibly be a teacher, so I began to look for a way to test it out.

A Gift Revealed

I told the Sunday School coordinators at my church that if they ever required a teacher, I would always have a lesson prepared. Their response – "How about this Sunday?" – took me by surprise. I swallowed hard as fear tightened every muscle in my throat. With eyes that must have looked as large as saucers, I squeaked out an "okay."

That first Sunday morning was a real thrill for me. Finally having an opportunity to share, through telling stories, some of the church history that I had been studying for years gave me a sense of accomplishment. In fact, many of those first ten people invited their friends. Before I knew it, there were over 100 people in the class. Soon there were invitations to speak and teach at other organizations throughout the Dallas/Fort Worth area.

When I began teaching my communications customers at the same time I was selling to them, my sales volume greatly increased. Not only did the knowledge of my primary internal gift enable me to become the coordinator for my division, it also gave me the opportunity to assist other people unlock their gifts and walk in their destiny.

There were also volunteer opportunities at The Road Adventure. Imagine being able to give back and bless people at the very place that had such an impact on me! The first weekend workshop I taught removed ANY doubt I had concerning the accuracy of my test result. At that moment, I was absolutely sure my primary internal gift was teaching. The excitement I felt when teaching was far greater than anything I experienced in my communications position.

I loved it so much that I began teaching as many workshops as possible at The Road Adventure. I would come home Sunday evening after teaching a three-day seminar with so much energy that I just had to tell my wife about all of the wonderful things that had happened that weekend. By 11:30 p.m. she was wondering how she was going to get me to be quiet so we could get some sleep. All I could think about was, "How can I do this tomorrow, and the next day, and the next?" I was so enthusiastic about this that I knew I had to find a way to make my passion my profession.

Turning My Passion into My Profession

In 2004, the opportunity to use my primary internal gift of teaching full time came: I was laid off. Okay, so maybe this was not the method I would have chosen for turning my passion into my profession, but I decided to take advantage of the opportunity anyway.

My favorite topics of sales, learning, and success, as well as assisting others served as the foundation for several workshops I created. My speaking and presenting experience enabled me to find outlets for these workshops.

A few months later, I heard that Zig Ziglar's organization was looking for presenters. The idea of working for his organization was both exciting and intimidating. The day after I sent them a demo DVD, I received an email with a contract offering me an opportunity to present Zig's material to others! Obviously, I accepted.

There is no way to describe the satisfaction that I got from being able to get paid for doing what I loved. My time with the Ziglar organization was a great experience and a time of growth for me. I began to realize that I knew a lot about sales, speaking, presenting, and teaching, but I knew very little about marketing. I suddenly recognized that marketing was the missing component to what I wanted to achieve in my life. Marketing knowledge would enable me to assist many more people than I had been able to assist so far.

As if that was not enough of an outlet for my primary internal gift of teaching, I also started my own radio show called *The Implementer's Corner*. (You can listen to several shows on www.PatrickDougher.com).

I might not have been the smartest person or the best student, but my achievements have surpassed many of those with higher academic skills because I took action. I was diligent and I surrounded myself with those who had the attitudes and skills that I wanted to develop.

After my second semester on academic probation, I implemented many of the accelerated learning techniques I teach today. By applying myself, I sowed the seeds of my current workshop entitled *Accelerated Learning – How to Learn Twice as Much in Half the Time* (available on both DVD and CD at www.GuaranteedBetterGrades.com).

Don't Just Survive – Thrive!

Knowing my primary internal gift has enabled me to have my own company. Before learning what my internal gift was, I merely *survived*. After learning my internal gift, I *thrived*. The more you know about how to harness your abilities, the more successful you'll be.

Mentors, coaches, and positive friends have made a huge difference in my life. Make sure you surround yourself with people who are overcomers. No matter how discouraging your circumstances are or what current skills you lack, there is hope. When you find your primary internal gift and start combining your natural talents with learned skills, life will become easier and more rewarding for you. Finding what I had to contribute to others has brought me great joy, as well as providing a full-time living for my family.

When you start to live out your destiny, you will have the joy of serving others, as well as the resulting financial rewards.

Because my life was so dramatically changed for the better as soon as I discovered my primary internal gift, I would like to bless you by assisting you to find these missing pieces in your own life. Please visit www.UsingYourInternalGifts.com for a free download on discovering your own personal internal gift so you, too, can manifest success!

Patrick Dougher is a gifted and passionate communicator who is widely sought after as a speaker, workshop presenter, mastermind group leader, and business coach. He exemplifies what he teaches in his workshop, Using Your Influence to Help Others Get What They Want in Life. Pat lives in Fort Worth, Texas with his wife and children. You can reach him at: pat@patrickdougher.com.

You Are Not
Your Business Card

You are not your business card. You are a person.

Attending a networking function can be a little like dating. Would you go out on a date, go to a restaurant, and before the waiter gets to the table to take your order, propose marriage to your date? Not likely. Yet for some reason that is exactly what we do at both social and business networking events. But we are not our business cards. Some people have the notion that once cards are exchanged, this ritual is a rite of passage not to do or say anything else. In truth, it's just a small piece of paper – smaller than a credit card – and has a street value of about a nickel. It's who *we* are that really matters, not what we *do*. Our hearts, not our business cards, are important.

It's what you stand for, not what you sell, that's relevant. It's not who you associate with, not where you live, or what vehicle you drive that defines you. It's *why* you do what you do that really counts. You are not your job – you are infinite opportunities, unlimited dreams, and ageless beauty. You are not a shark in a suit; you are an eagle with wings.

The Real Deal

Who am I? I'm just a just guy who woke up this morning at 4:00 a.m. and realized that most of us have been hypnotized at an early age, and as adults we have remained in this hypnotic state. For good reason we were taught not to talk to strangers, so we paid attention. We became cautious,

69

less curious. We locked our doors; we closed our minds. We put on the armor of the "right business suit." We went out and got business cards, and we communicate by phone and email – yes, even to the people sitting in the same room – both at home and at the office.

My wake-up call? We are not children – we *can* talk to strangers. We can get to know the person at the checkout line, the bus, the train, the plane, and the bagel shop. People do not do business with business cards; they do business with people. So maybe the real question is not what type style or color you should use on your business card. Maybe the real question is, "Who are you?" What do you stand for? Why do you do what you do?" By the way, these questions are frightening – terrifying. But these are the real questions, the real deal. Are *you* the real deal?

Too many people follow what I call the "family of origin script" and live a life not their own. Living the "family of origin" script is comfortable, safe, and secure. In truth, it's a prison – three "hots and a cot," as they say in prisons. Leaving this place takes courage. Courage is not being fearless; courage is moving forward while facing your fear, period.

Our real fear is not of failure. Our real fear is of possibility, of what we are, of what we may become. Our real fear is that glimpse of amazing abundance, infinite wisdom, and boundless possibilities. We fear ourselves and our possibilities.

Own Your Own Journey

Within each of us is a seed, a seed that must be planted, nurtured, cultivated, and embraced. It's *your* seed – not your mom's, your dad's, your teachers, your preachers, or your neighbor's. You own it, and you are responsible for its outcome. If we allow others to direct, dictate, and manage us in an all-out effort not to take ownership of our lives, we avoid the ownership of the outcome. We lose by default no matter how large our portfolio, the value of our estate, or the size of our business.

Never live by default. Plant your own your seed, own your journey, and celebrate the ownership of your outcome. Remind yourself that every day above ground is a great one; it's a gift, so be thankful.

When I first started my journey, I wrote the following poem. Since then, I have not used a business card, even though I have completed over 6,000 speaking events, over 100 consulting assignments, and counseled over 1,000,000 people. I am not my business card!

> *We are born complete;*
> > *we are not born deficient.*
> *We need not be fixed,*
> > *for we are not broken.*
> *We are whole,*
> > *not fragmented.*
> *We need to nurture the child in us,*
> > *not force it to grow up.*
> *We are love,*
> > *only love.*
> *It is fear that prevents us from*
> *being who we really are.*
> *We are love,*
> > *only love.*

Ted Fattoross is the CEO and founder of the following organizations: TedSpeak.com, joinnetworksplus.com, Safe School Foundation, Ebony & Ivory, and Educational Services. Ted is blessed to be Daddy to both Taylor and Jared and the son of Muriel and Vincent. Ted guarantees to exceed his clients' expectations and can be reached at TedFatrossCEO@ joinnetworkplus.com or 201-933-5235.

 *Manifest Success*

Caryn Gottlieb-FitzGerald

L'Chaim
"To Life"

From the day we are born, to the day we die, we live by the power of intention.

It took me three decades to realize how powerful and true that statement is. Why is it that I choose to create such difficulty in my world for the first three decades of my life? I had not realized how simple it was to create goals and dreams within my own mind, focus on the outcome, not concern myself with "how" it will happen, and trust enough to let the Universe provide. I now know, on a very deep level, I was asking for assistance for my life to change and to be able to live the life I truly deserved and desired. This request was in my heart, the desire to change the misery I was living day to day was so strong that the Universe had no other option but to answer my request. From that day forth my life was forever changed. If I close my eyes I can feel the emotional heat within my body, the wetness of the tears streaming down my face, and the pounding of my head on that warm spring day in Dallas, as I first heard the words that would forever change my life.

Growing up, my family was mildly dysfunctional and pretty common. My parents divorced when I was ten. By the time I was fourteen, we had lived in several places, finally settling in sunny south Florida. To me, it seemed that life was always a challenge. What I did not know then was that the reason life was a challenge was directly related to the thoughts I had racing through my mind, creating my reality. Although I was successful in almost everything I chose to do, I found that as I moved towards success I would sabotage myself, guaranteeing failure.

73

Being organized and in control were always part of my life. I was so focused on being in control that the world I had created for myself was filled with negativity, abuse, and an overwhelming sadness. This was most evident in my relationships with men. At 16, I met an amazing guy who treated me like a queen, yet my lack of self-worth led me to sabotage things enough that the relationship ended. By 18, I found myself in the first of several relationships with older men who were controlling and abusive.

Positive self-esteem is very important for young women, and something I was lacking. I clearly remember sharing my thoughts about being "overweight" with "Jack", a man I dated on and off for many years and who tried to teach me that physical abuse was acceptable when you love someone. Although I was not overweight, I was sensitive about my size all through school. Most of the females around me were dancers and cheerleaders, so they were very petite in size. I spent my free time biking and swimming, so my physique was much different and at five foot seven, I felt I looked huge against to my friends. This was something that coursed through me for many years. "Jack" encouraged me to diet, which led to weight loss and within one year spiraled me into an eating disorder that had its roots firmly grounded in 18 years of my past. Ironically, I became so consumed by my illness that the relationship ended, saving me from his physical abuse.

I transitioned from a physically abusive relationship into an emotionally abusive relationship with "Dirk", a man over a decade older than me. From the outside he appeared to be as close to perfect as any man could be. Women would fawn over him and treat him as if he was some type of godlike creature and when things were good, he was caring, loving, and had a twinkle in his eyes that could turn any woman's head. On the dark side, he had a nasty temper that lead to many heated arguments. He used my weaknesses against me, and I admit I did the same. After two years of dating, exchanging "I Love You's," fighting and making up, he floored me one day by calling to say he was marrying someone else.

He simply informed me that halfway through our relationship, he had met someone else, however she did not believe in premarital sex, so he continued our relationship which included sex for another year while they developed a relationship that ultimately lead to marriage. It did not disappoint me to learn this marriage lasted less than a week. However he knew my weaknesses as I allowed him to return to my life a short time later, and intertwine himself into my world for years to come.

On the outside, I appeared to be a well-adjusted, fun-loving individual. Yet, under the facade was sadness, fear, and a deep-seated desire for something different, something more, to have an abundant life filled with loving, caring individuals. These underlying desires were strong enough to bring a wonderful man into my circle and after realizing that his love was true and real, I allowed myself to accept that he was someone I deserved.

We married and I spent the first part of our marriage hiding my illness from him. With time, I accepted that he was not leaving, that his love was true, and no hidden "dark side" of abuse was coming to the surface. I began to relax, and after spending ten years consumed by an eating disorder that brought me to the brink of death before my thirtieth birthday, the light finally began to shine in my life. My focus was now on my desire to live, to be truly happy and to create a world where I was surrounded by individuals like my husband, people who truly cared and supported me. I decided I was no longer going to allow anorexia and bulimia to consume me. I understood that my illness was not only ravaging my body, as I stood five foot seven and weighed barely one hundred and five pounds, but it was ravaging my mind, my soul, and the very core of my being. I decided I was going to live, and live within the world I desired for myself. This was the first experience I can remember with setting a goal and achieving it by focusing on the outcome and not being concerned with *how* it would happen. All I knew was that I was going to survive and thrive.

For the next few years I lived in what I felt was a good place for me. I was surrounded by people I called friends and loved ones who cared deeply for me. However, I still had that yearning desire for more. I was lacking fulfillment and at times still felt an empty sadness. I was not able to describe why the feeling was there, I just knew that there was more waiting for me, that my journey was far from over. I had steps to take and inner demons to fight, all things that required time and attention for me to move forward. I knew that to live the lifestyle I desired I had to ask; but I was lacking the skills in which to continue the process.

Then, on that warm spring day in Dallas, I found myself listening to someone else's story of growth and change, and I realized I was receiving the answers as to where I would find the skills I required to continue on my journey. As I heard her story, I felt my chest tighten, my stomach twist in knots, and my head began to pound, as there was a familiarity in what she was expressing, my eyes filled with tears as she shared that there was a light at the end of the tunnel, that life did not have to be so difficult. For the first time, I realized that I was not alone, nor was I unique in feeling that life seemed so challenging. Her story resonated through my core as the answers I had been searching for were now being brought to me. I was now listening as my inner voice told me that this connection would lead me through the next steps in my journey. With tears streaming down my face, my heart racing, and my body filled with fear of the unknown, I stepped forward...

Caryn Gottlieb-FitzGerald is an author and professional speaker who has been sharing her love of the written word for over 25 years. Caryn resides in Texas with her husband and daughter. She is the author of "Tulips in the Sand ~ A Riley Matthews Mystery" and proudly co-authored a gratitude workbook for children in 2007 with her 6-year-old daughter, Sami FitzGerald. For more information please visit: http://www.CarynFitzGerald.com.

Expanding Your Vision to Action

Many years I ago I learned firsthand the major difference between a dream and vision. The reality that I came up with shocked me. They are in fact one in the same. Life without action leads to a lonely town called nowhere. You may have visited this place a time or two.

If you have ever been there it will leave you feeling unfulfilled. It leaves you uncertain about yourself and your existence. It does not empower you by staying there. The longer you stay there it actually weakens you. It sucks the life right out of you until you become numb to it and the other people stuck there. Key #1: Stop! (Wake up). Key#2: Release! (Let go of your weak thoughts). Key#3: Action! (Discover what means the most to you and go for it). This process reminds me of when I was 9 years old learning how to fire a rifle. Ready! Aim! Fire!

However, there is a special place on this earth for those who take these simple steps. If you are truly ready to create the life you deserve then I'm speaking directly to you. Listen closely because this information once applied will inspire you to do the many powerful, great things you once visioned. No time to waste let us begin...

YOU! Yes, YOU! Don't look around, it's just you and me here. I want your full attention. I am specifically talking about a major transformation from a talker to a doer.

Just talking about the action steps inspires me to go beyond anything I once thought I couldn't do. You and I connecting right here, right now, was once a dream of mine. To assist 10's of thousands of people all around the globe was my vision. By tapping into my own unbreakable human spirit, life has given me the juice and joy to pursue and manifest some finest moment. I can clearly contest to the fact that the more I reach, the more I CAN reach, which you will discover for yourself once this information is applied.

What I'm about to uncover for you can change your life. Just don't read this and tell yourself that was nice or interesting. Keep in mind this is coming from someone who has been homeless, broke, without a car, etc. who one day decided to explore his purpose. Let me tell you the results may shock you.

This is where all the magic resides. It will always be there and welcome you back. Your life is really waiting you to find its purpose, are your ready to unleash it? Let's go for it!

Ask yourself, how will this information serve me?

This information will dramatically serve you, provided you take the actions necessary, but you will never take the actions necessary if your vision is not extraordinary. In order for your vision to be extraordinary, you must posses extraordinary thoughts, you must possess extraordinary dreams. This is the starting point. Yes, stop what you're doing for a second or two and decide if you're really striving for ordinary or extraordinary goals.

Let me tell you a secret. It is much easier to have extraordinary goals than ordinary goals. How is that possible? The subconscious has communication with the conscious and they grade talk with each other about how far are you willing to stretch. If you settle for ordinary goals your subconscious get bored and feels neglected and losses interest in assisting you with the answers you really want to create. Never under estimate the power of your subconscious and consious mind once it gets excited.

By doing so, you will possess extraordinary powers for the use of your faith muscles know as actions. Goal getting is the ultimate achievement. I had a mentor who was a self made billionaire once tell if me, if you are going to dream, dream big. You must possess extraordinary goals, if your goals are minuet, I guarantee your actions are going to be minuet. If it does not get you out of your comfort zone, nothing will ever change. So this info will serve you because it will change you and other people around you for a lifetime provided that you get in the game and play well and don't ever quit. Persistence is the key that starts this engine of expanding your vision to action.

What must I do for peak results?

First, expand your vision by connecting your ideas with other people. You MUST get completely out of your comfort zone....The distance away from your comfort zone will only be measured by the faith one has in themselves to complete the task at hand. Unwavering faith is the applied faith you must have with a burning desire for your goals. Your ultimate goals are waiting for you to reach for them. They will not be handed to you. You earn them by going beyond that which you think was once possible. Operating by faith and not absolutes. Clearing the mental mechanism. A mind that is distracted is a mind that is defeated.

Stop the worrying. 92% of what people worry about never happens and the main reason people fail in life is because nobody knows about them or their passion. How many people have you shared your vision with today? How many listened? How many referrals did you obtain? Did you ask for any? Connecting with the right people is imperative.

The second important plan for you in obtaining peak results is keeping track of your progress and activity. A precious asset you have that must not be dealt with lightly is your time. The time you invest doing verses thinking will pay the greatest dividends. So invest wisely and always keep track. Know your game plan. The things you will be doing tomorrow, day by day, hour by hour, week by week and month by month. Create value for the things you desire the most and place laser focus on its attainment. Track everything. Know if what you're doing is serving you. You will get the most out of your 24 hours if you do just that.

Lastly, fine tune your mind to an unwavering skill set. Don't wish attaining your goals were easier, wish your creative vision and actions were better. Always lead with a positive mental attitude. Carry with you at all times a no limitations believe. As you read this understand the possibilities for everyone are only bounded by the mind. Never let people steal your dream. It's your dream and your right to do whatever you desire.

As a final note for you:

Never lose your sense of wonder. In order to explore new oceans, you must be willing to take your eyes off the shore. Focus all your action towards operating from possibility vs. limits. This will be where you grow. Understanding what you've done to this point in your life and how to Breakthrough to Wealth and Mastery is a matter of uncommon thoughts. The thoughts you think reflect the actions you take. Ultimately they render the results you obtain. This is where we let your experience operating from possibility verses limits take charge.

90% of all failure comes from quitting! NEVER! EVER! Quit! Your dreams are counting on you to manifest them!

From his humble beginnings growing up in the valley of California, **Randy Gonzales Jr.** grew up with the understanding of taking action at an early age. In his 14-year journey he has transitioned from virtually unseen and unheard of, to become a highly demanded speaker, results coach, and published author. His simple, yet highly effective, way of thinking triggers people to take action. Millionaire Partnerships, Inc. www. millionairepartnerships.com.

Manifest Success

Shirley La Barre

Epiphany

Challenging events and people can change our lives forever....

Epiphany has become a buzzword. Perhaps a more definitive term would be *insight* or possibly, *wisdom*. I know I have seen lives changed by some experience – an accident, a death, a change of location or job, or often, a spiritual awakening. One certainty is that life is not limited by one or even two life-changing happenings. It is an ongoing process where different people, as well as just happenstance, affect our lives.

I am in my eighties, and people and events parade across my memory like those students of several generations saying goodbye to Mr. Chips. However, two important events stand like road markers along my journey.

A Test of Faith

I can't remember a time when I did not believe Jesus Christ was my Savior. Admittedly, I perceived God as a cross between my mother and Santa Claus: I knew I would be punished for naughtiness and I was sure God could part seas, move mountains, and care for my soul. A life-changing test came one family vacation at the end of January.

We hadn't had a holiday since our third son had been born six months before, so we took a week in the mountains to play in the snow. A pleasant cottage allowed us a week of sledding, tobogganing, and violent snowball battles. An evening snowfall was a gift that we hadn't expected.

When it was time to return home, we waited until rather late so the baby would sleep. Our older boys (ages seven and five) were told to push the stroller along the road in front while we packed. They were dressed lightly for the trip. I came out, carrying stuff, and didn't see the children. I asked my husband if he had permitted them to go someplace, and his "no" set my alert button screaming. We ran both directions on the dirt road. There was silence. Panic replaced fear, and I said, "Do you think they could have gone down to the pier?" Loren, calmness personified, immediately got in the car. We found stroller tracks leading down to the wooden pier, but no sight of the children.

We both ran to the ranger's office to ask for help. The ranger responded to our anxious explanation and grabbed his heavy coat and a rifle. I cried, "Why do you need that?" The ranger didn't answer, but put his hand on my shoulder and urged Loren to have me return to the car in case the children came that way, but I heard him say quietly that it was too late to get a helicopter, as it would soon be dark and the bears had just come out!

I tried to be calm, but on my return to the car, I was teetering on hysteria. Loren tucked me in a blanket, held my face in his hand, and said, "I'll find them. I promise I will."

Why didn't I make them wear their snow clothes? How could they disappear so fast? Could they have been kidnapped? Where were they?

Outside the car the shadows lengthened and then were gone. A light snow began to fall. "Oh, God," I cried, "Please let them be found!" I bargained. "If only you bring them back, I won't ever leave them on their own again." I forget any other deals I offered. God was not Santa Claus, and I fell back on my juvenile faith: the blessed assurance that God could DO anything. I summoned that spiritual force and finally begged, "Oh, God, your will be done, but please could you let me have one back?"

84

There was no sound and no peace. Bending over in complete surrender I said, "I give up, Lord. I surrender to your complete will."

Unable to look at the dark emptiness, I barely heard the door open as Loren handed me our baby, while two cold, silent little boys climbed in the back seat. Uncontrollable sobbing and tears exploded from me. I felt a pair of little arms wind around my neck, and Jeffrey, the oldest, said, "Don't cry, Mama. I told Doug that I knew Daddy would find us and get us out!"

That seven-year-old's faith in his dad became a touchtone in my life. It seems Jeffrey had wanted to see the sledding slope again and thought he knew a short cut to the cabin. But the trail grew narrow, and the stroller tires froze in the snow. Their dad found them on the edge of a steep drop to a canyon below.

There have been other times that life has brought seemingly insurmountable problems, and over and again I have known that my father, God, would get me through.

A Writer Is Born

There have been many people who have influenced my life choices, sometimes profoundly. A very close friend began college and encouraged me to come along. We enrolled at UCLA. There had been teachers along the way who suggested writing as a career, and several professors who urged me to write and publish.

When I got my credentials, I began teaching at a new school with outstanding students. I was to teach twelfth grade students in English, and I was also given an honors class. I encouraged and urged and even tutored some gifted students, and they did publish, some while still in high school. I said, "Start now, and even if you wallpaper your bedroom with rejection slips, do it!"

But what about me? No, I never even risked a submission of *my* writing, even though I had a file of poems and articles. Then, at the close of a week of special meetings led by Oz Guinness that my husband and I were attending, Oz challenged each of us to do something we had always wanted to do. We wrote down a pledge that would be returned in four months.

I had recently retired, and I was sixty years old. Could I? I took the risk and ended up selling my submitted article three times. I was even asked to contribute more articles. Later, a group I belonged to urged me to publish a collection of poems that I had shared with them. I did. When I volunteered to help at our church, I was asked to be an editor of the newsletter. I also contributed to a quarterly magazine for new writers, as well as write articles for the city newspaper.

When we moved from our home of forty-seven years to a small town north of Los Angeles, I was sixty-nine, and I thought my writing for publications was over. Not so. Always an ardent gardener, I was asked to write a monthly column for the newspaper. I also wrote a series of interviews with members of the community who had been residents for a long time. Later, I published a book on the history of the Ojai Presbyterian Church, so rich in history for nearly 200 years that it required many months of research. It has been my favorite writing venture thus far.

I am now writing a collection of memoirs of the first seven years of my life to be called *The Chinaberry Tree*. Dear Oz Guinness never dreamt that his challenge gave me a whole new life of purpose. I pursue it with joy with whatever time I have left to live, to write, and to serve.

Epiphany

In spite of spending years teaching and encouraging students to write for publication, **Shirley La Barre**'s first published writings were as the editor of a monthly alumni magazine and contributions to a collection of local writers. She has a published book of poetry and one on the history of the Ojai Presbyterian Church, as well as many monthly gardening articles. Shirley is presently writing her remembrances of the first seven years of her life in Arizona.

Manifest Success

Monaica Ledell

Being Top Heavy

People always ask me how I've achieved so much at a young age. When I was growing up, my father always used to say, *"Monaica, you just always land on your feet."* (Thanks for planting that in my subconscious mind, Dad!) He was right back then, and he's still right. Not only do I always land on my feet, but I always seem to land on top – even in the face of seeming disaster.

I'm a strategist, what can I say? When new opportunities come into my life, it's like I revert back to being four years old watching someone flash a juicy piece of candy in front of my face. Achieving the end result, capitalizing on the opportunity, finishing the race…all of those things become obsessions, and I refuse to stop until I reach the end goal.

The Decision to Change

But, once upon a time, due to a series of foolish decisions I made, you could have summed up my life by visualizing a Port-A-Potty. Every halfway decent opportunity I had been handed I managed to either destroy or sabotage, including a scholarship to the fifteenth best university in the United States, a few "good" jobs, and a full bank account. As my days became more riddled with fear, I felt as if I were literally suffocating. One penniless morning, I woke up and made a decision that I was no longer going to live this way. I finally began to ask for some assistance. When you don't have anywhere else to go God seems likes the only answer. Almost instantaneously, people came into my life that assisted me to get to the next place, take the next step, or teach me something imperative to my success. I will be forever grateful to those selfless angels for lovingly directing me home.

Looking back, I can see that the key was my willingness to change how I had been viewing myself, the world, God, spirituality, my past, and my future. When you've broken down by the side of the road without a phone, and there are no other cars in sight, it's easy to become willing to learn how to change a tire. When you've squandered enough opportunities, it becomes much easier to accept that you must change your perception of life and the world.

My father always taught me that experiencing God's grace was not God zooming down to earth on his white cloud with his crew of angels like Santa Claus and his twelve reindeer. He would say, "Honey, experiencing the grace of God is when God gives you an opportunity to change…but whether or not you take it is entirely up to you. Just remember, kid, you don't know when your opportunities are going to run out…."

Those words haunted me until the morning I made the DECISION to change everything. I made a decision to say "yes" to being true to me and following the passions that I had locked away.

I had been trying to be something I was not. If I *thought* someone wanted me to be a certain way, then I would act that way. If you've ever suffered from "trying-to-be-something-you-are-not-ism," then you know that it becomes exhausting. I became the colors of the chameleon, changing what I thought others wanted me to change in order to feel more secure. I was too scared to be me. I was losing a part of myself each time I took action on those feelings, and I never gained true security.

Aligned and Authentic

What are you currently doing in your life that is not in alignment with your authentic self? Are you in a job because you're afraid of what others will think if you do something different? Did you choose a profession (based on trying to fill your own insecurities) so that others would be "proud" of you? Did you get married because you thought it was the thing to do, or because you had really found your soul mate?

Not only was I not living my truths, but I was following the dictates based on what I thought was happening in society. My perception was totally off base; every day I would get up and measure your outsides with my insides. It took many failures for me to be courageous enough to admit that I was a phony!

When I was ready to see and admit the truth, doors immediately started opening, and my beliefs about failure changed. I used to feared failure the most, whereas now I realize it's simply a stop on life's journey, where I get to learn more about myself than I would from my successes! I invite failure today because I know that I will learn the secrets to achieving my goals.

Steps to Becoming Top Heavy

If you want to become "top heavy" in your life, it's really pretty simple:

> *Look for opportunities. Listen - they are always knocking.*
> *Be your best. If you don't give your best, how can you expect to get the gold medal?*
> *Accept that there will be difficult circumstances you will have to navigate around – become one with your internal GPS tracker...Om...).*

Keep it fun. Laugh a lot. If you can't find a way to make whatever you're doing fun, then you've just shot yourself in the foot. Life is not a dress rehearsal – we only have one shot at this! I'm personally inviting you to come to my "Life Is Fun" party.

Make GOOD DECISIONS, and quick ones, whenever possible. Don't allow your past into the present moment. When you make a wrong decision, simply make a new decision.

Be honest. This typically doesn't come easy for most of us. Honesty is a learned skill to work towards.

Be grateful for both the good times and the not so good times. When you can be thankful for the worst times in your life, the gifts that follow are amazing.

Align yourself with your passions. Do what you love. If you must do something you're not totally in love with, keep your focus on your passion and find that piece of it you can love. Love, happiness, and fun have no size requirements.

Believe in yourself. If you can't do that, find out why, and then work towards gaining exponential power and strength through remembering who you really are.

There are no real secrets to being "top heavy." The most successful people in the world are no more special than you or me, nor do they belong to a secret society where they privately discuss strategies to leave the little people behind. They are just more consistent at doing the above nine steps. Let discipline and the consistency of making good decisions assist you to reach your goals. You will find that achieving what you desire can be done with grace and ease; daily living can be full of happiness, exhilaration, and pure fun. *What else would life be for?*

Young. Passionate. Modern. Successful. Coach. Business Strategist. Creative Genius. **Monaica Ledell** is a modern young entrepreneur who has already accomplished a great deal in her life. A million-dollar business strategist, Monaica teaches other young (and old) entrepreneurs how to use modernized strategies to break through marketing noise. Leverage and automate your business, and live a rich and fulfilling life. You can learn more about Monaica by visiting www.modernandmillions.com.

Trevor Lovell

Are You Ready
to Be An Entrepreneur?

"Those that dare to dream during their waking hours shape the world"
-Mr. Mozone

Are you thinking about going into business for yourself? Do you wish that you had had the courage to do so when the opportunity presented itself? Are you really ready to become your own boss?

Being an entrepreneur is the most satisfying adventure life has to offer. It's also the scariest because the only person you are accountable to is yourself. Success becomes your boss. If you don't get up in the morning and breathe life into your enterprise, the money flow stops and failure takes over. I know this firsthand! I have now come full circle with my inner demons, allowing me to live in prosperity and educate others about money.

Live with Passion

A common thread that binds all entrepreneurs is passion. If you have passion, you will have money flowing to you. If there is no passion, money won't flow and you won't be successful. Martin Luther King, Jr. stated, "Most men die at twenty-one, we just don't bury them until sixty-five." This is the unfortunate way many live their lives today. I was there too, and by making a conscious decision, I am now living with passion and sharing this gift with others.

My passion comes from my competiveness to help others win. I have learned that in order to be successful I must give first and be open to receiving second. This game of life is not all about me, and as soon as I learned to accept and understand this part of the game, my life began to flourish. My biggest challenge was being universally selfish, to myself, my family, and in business. Being in business became my sport, and by living with the mentality of winning at all costs, I lost far more than I gained, in both business and personal relationships. I was only briefly profitable. In business, I was always challenged to increase revenues, and at times I sacrificed my business philosophy for immediate profit. In my personal relationships, I experienced anger, hurt, and frustration when those I was dealing with did not agree that it was all about me. I finally had to step back and take a good, unbiased look at what I was doing, where I was in life, and who I was destined to become if changes were not made. The hardest step I ever took was leaving my old self behind and moving forward into my new self, with new beliefs, new attitudes, new goals, and a new focus of assisting others before myself.

Embrace New Beliefs

One of my new beliefs is that being successful as a business owner is when I am able to walk away from daily business obligations and still have large sums of money flowing into my bank accounts on a daily basis. I now know I can achieve this by simply assisting others to succeed. I achieve my goals faster by assisting others to reach their goals, and the more people I assist, the bigger successes happen for all involved. Keep in mind that my definition of success may be different from yours, and your definition may be different from those around you. The important thing is that you have a personal definition of success. It should fill your heart and soul with passion. The desire for success should be so great that it flows through every part of your body on a constant basis until achieved.

It is common for entrepreneurs to face controversy within their circle of family and friends because most people never dare to take action on their dreams, and those that do make others feel nervous and uncertain. Rest assured, as you move forward your circle of influence will change. Those filled with negativity will fall away as those filled with positive energy will replace them in your life.

Take Action

As entrepreneurs, those we mentor require a leader who will lead by doing and not just by telling, and this will be evident in their actions. For example, the other day at a restaurant, while we were waiting to be seated my eleven-year-old daughter began speaking to a middle-aged couple and their daughter. She was asking them questions about their lives with the goal of enticing them to our business, as we help individuals and families to increase their wealth. After a few moments the wife told my daughter that she should not talk to strangers. My daughter responded by politely asking, "How do you make friends if you do not talk to people?" Interesting question, I thought. My daughter saw something in that couple and took action without concerning herself with what their limiting beliefs might have been. I am proud of the way she did what she has seen me do thousands of times; taking action where I felt action was required. By taking action she moved closer to the success she desires. The opportunity is presented and it is then up to the individual to accept or decline the invitation. We can only move forward with the best of intention, knowing others will receive only what they choose to receive.

As an entrepreneur, your challenge is to embrace the process with its ups and downs. It starts with the willingness to accept a shift in your belief system. Do not be fooled into thinking that this will be an easy road – the reality is that it is easier to stay in the same cycle day after day and not take action. Taking a step forward requires the courage to move through the fear of the unknown. My mentor has a saying, "What you do not hate you begin to tolerate."

Dream It – Live It

Remember, never take advice from someone that is not where you desire to be. Listen to those that have been where you are and have moved forward to achieve the successes you desire. Dream about how great it will feel to be to your own boss, to have the luxury of time to do what you want to do, to be who you want to be. Dream it, feel it, and live it within your body and soul, and it will become reality for you. I enjoy the pleasure I receive in never having to ask another adult for permission to go on a family vacation or asking for time off to see my child's sporting event. It makes me feel great to know that only I control my time now, and no one else will ever be able to tell me differently.

Being an entrepreneur is about teaching and educating people about how the game is played. The goal is to introduce positive life strategies to individuals who otherwise would have missed out on the growth opportunities available on a daily basis. Dreams can be as large or as small as we desire. Goals of any magnitude can be achieved regardless of where we come from. I am a dreamer who has learned to transition his childhood dream into the biggest game of all. And I'm thankful for my parents who always told me, "Don't let life happen to you – you make life happen."

Trevor Lovell is committed to learning, personal growth, and a deep desire to make others around him better by striving to be the best in all he does. He is a financial planner/financial professional. He is a loving and caring father. Trevor's commitment to integrity lifts him head and shoulders above the average and ordinary. Feel free to contact him at NRinvestor@gmail.com.

Carol Mason

Using No as a Stepping Stone to Success

I grew up in Chappaqua, New York. Chappaqua is an affluent suburb twenty-five miles north of New York City where I was exposed to pretty much any opportunity you can think of. I was accustomed to the good things in life, and this made me desire to attain all of this and more when I became an adult. Even as a young girl, I always dreamed big. I would daydream of being a super model and having my photo taken by all the important magazines, being a professional athlete competing in the Olympics, or a multimillionaire being chauffeured around in a limousine. I always knew that one day I would be successful, no matter what other people's thought of me. My parents always encouraged me to pursue my dreams and never stood in my way.

My first dream at the age of twelve was being a professional tennis player. Since I started playing tennis when I was eleven at the age most people considered too late for professional competition, all I heard was that I could never be good enough to turn pro and shouldn't waste my time and effort. I wasn't going to let that stop me. My dream was like the bull's-eye on a dartboard. My determination and focus was piercing. I was going to be a top player, no matter what sacrifices were required. I trained daily after school, went to weekly tennis lessons given by a top Australian coach, and played in a tournament practically every weekend.

A Vital Lesson

Along the way my tennis coach, Alan Lane, taught me a vital lesson that I still utilize to this day. He taught me to look in the mirror every morning and tell myself, "I love who I am," as well as additional positive statements such as, "You are a great tennis player, and you will win matches. You have the potential to be the best tennis player ever." If you follow this lesson as well you will be amazed at the way your subconscious mind changes its way of thinking, and you will start to see results. You have to love yourself before others can love you. You have to be grateful for all that you have before the universe will send more your way.

I spent the next few years playing in tournaments, and I achieved a top ranking on the East Coast. To date, I am the first and only female tennis player at Horace Greeley High School to go to the New York state finals. I played #1 singles for my high school and rarely lost a match. During my senior year I was approached by a sports agent who presented me with multiple full tennis scholarships to colleges I dreamed of attending. I'm not telling you this to brag, but rather to show you an example of how I overcame years of nos and never gave up. If you put your mind to something and stay focused, you too can achieve great things.

After playing college tennis for two years I knew I wanted to turn pro. This meant finding a sponsor to pay for everything. This is a tough task because sponsors pay for private coaching, entry fees to tournaments all around the world, and all travel expenses, which can amount to a minimum of $100,000. I cannot tell you how many wealthy individuals and corporations told me no. Desperate and determined, I proceeded to get dressed in my tennis best, printed out my tennis resume, and began to drive around to the wealthiest neighborhoods. I knocked on homeowners' doors and gave them my speech.

One day I got the courage to call Nick Bollettieri, who coaches some of the world's top tennis players and was always on TV. People thought I was crazy calling someone so famous. Nick told me he was coming to

New York for the U.S. Open and would watch me play, and if he thought I had potential he would sponsor me. Well, I played my heart out, and he said yes! I can't imagine my life today if I hadn't made the decision to pick up the phone and make that call. Taking that risk gave me the reward of playing on the pro tour for four and a half years and traveling all over the world. Even though I didn't reach the top 100 world rankings, I am proud of what I achieved. Even though all along I kept hearing how I would never achieve my dream, how nobody would sponsor me, how I started too late, etc., I made it happen and nobody can take that away from me. I learned how to channel those nos into finding that one yes. It was my perseverance that changed my life forever.

New Dreams

I stopped playing tennis when I was twenty-four years old and proceeded to my next dream in life, the dream of working on a trading floor. When I began to interview I was often told that I didn't have the appropriate degree or family connections to get the position. I decided to accept a junior position, which I'm sure most people would snub their noses at, but at least I was working on the trading floor. I now had access to people who made decisions. I worked on the bond-trading floor, where there were only five women out of 500 employees. I asked the senior manager every single week if I could be given the opportunity to interview along with all the other men for an opening, and every week he told me no. He also told me that it was never going to happen, and that I should just accept it and quit.

This went on for the next year and a half – until finally one time he said yes! There were twenty-five candidates that interviewed for a retail government sales position, and I was offered the job! Again, even though for a year and a half all I heard was no, I kept believing in my dream. I knew one day I would finally be told yes. I often wonder how my life would have been different if I gave up right before the opportunity was offered. I often hear of people quitting days before their big break would have happened.

Back to the Corporate Grind

After five years working on the trading floor I moved to London, got married, and had my son Christopher. I then stayed home with my son for eight years and was content being the best mother I could be. Unfortunately, my marriage ended and I got a divorce. By then we had moved back to the U.S., and in order for my son to stay in the wonderful school system we cherished, I had no choice but to go back to work. Back to the corporate world I went. Back to a long commute, sixty-hour workweeks, stressful days, and constant rushing. Most importantly, I missed being home with my son. After dedicating myself to a top global bank for nine years, I was laid off without so much as a thank you. That's when I made the decision that I wouldn't go back into the corporate world; I had enough. I made the choice that I was going to be an entrepreneur and start building my own castle once again. I would find a home-based business that would enable me to stay home with my son and give me control of my finances and my future.

Success Is a Choice

When I shared my decision with my fellow coworkers, they told me I was crazy, that it was too risky, and that all home-based businesses were scams. I realized they were afraid of taking the risk, and I didn't listen to their advice. After looking at many businesses, I joined Wealth Masters International. I now spend all the time I want with my son, work from the comfort of my home, and earn more money than I did in the corporate world. I have surrounded myself with like-thinking minds and fellow entrepreneurs with the same goal in life.

I will leave you with a thought. Success is a choice. If you don't make a decision today, then nothing will ever change tomorrow. Believe in yourself, stopping listening to the nos, and say yes to the lifestyle of your dreams!

Carol Mason is a former professional tennis player and Wall Street employee, single mother of her amazing son Christopher, and currently a successful home-based business entrepreneur. In 2007, she made the decision to take control of her finances and her future, and joined Wealth Masters International. To find out more about WMI's products, go to www. wmitoday.com/mort13, www.TopBiz4Wealth.com, or feel free to email Carol at mason1960@aol.com. You can also visit Carol's blog: www. carolmason.blogspot.com.

Manifest Success

All the Riches You Haven't Recognized or Claimed in the Past Are Still Available to You

At lunch the other day, Lisa, a client of mine, was complaining that she'd had a brilliant idea for an e-book, but someone else "stole" it and created an e-book on the same topic that wasn't as good as hers would have been. This author's e-book was tremendously successful, and Lisa felt that he'd destroyed any possibility of hers becoming successful.

"That e-book was my one big chance, and he blew it out of the water," she complained.

I said, "I think that was a big chance for you, not your 'one' big chance. If you came up with an idea as fabulous as that one, I'm sure you can come up with another."

Lisa looked at me sceptically, and I know what she was thinking: *There are no second chances*. Well, I don't believe that for a minute. I believe that if we open ourselves up to possibility and trust in the abundant, giving Universe, we'll have second, third, fourth, and 3,832nd chances! Look around, and you'll see examples of people who reinvented their lives and went from rags to riches, to rags to riches again.

"Maybe you weren't meant to write that particular e-book," I told Lisa. "Or maybe you were meant to write it, but in a different way, in your own voice – and it's going to be a much bigger success than you imagine. Or maybe it's not meant to be a book, but a business, a Web site, or something else."

Unlimited Opportunities

I told her about a friend of mine who was approached by an editor to write a book on a particular topic. She created a book proposal that the editor loved, but his boss wouldn't let him acquire the book, reasoning that my friend's take on the topic was too lighthearted to sell well in the marketplace. She proceeded to have a dozen publishers turn the book down before one signed it, and it went on to generate five sequels and sell a quarter of a million copies in a half dozen languages. The book even inspired a television show based on her lighthearted content. Her "one big chance" seemed to have passed her by when that first publisher said no, but she chose to believe in second chances and an abundance of opportunities.

The Universe wants to give to you. The moment you begin to change your vibration to one of abundance, it will start sending you people, situations, and opportunities that reflect your inner state. You'll start to see possibilities for wealth creation, whether they're the exact ones you failed to notice previously or new ones.

It can be difficult to let go of the feeling of *I blew it!* and watch as others enjoy the riches that passed you by. Some friends of mine were trading stories once, and everyone had a family chronicle about "Uncle Theo," who sold that gorgeous brick home for a song without telling his brother, and now it's worth a fortune . . . or of Great-Grandpa, who was too skittish to buy up beachfront property years ago and watched his best friend who did invest become a self-made millionaire, while he continued to work in the grocery store. As everyone told their family's tale, we had to laugh, because for all the lost chances, here we were, years later, enjoying tremendous abundance together.

Would any of us really be all that much happier if that relative long ago didn't make what seemed like a "disastrous" mistake at the time? I doubt it!

The Door to Abundance Is Never Locked

Over the years, I've heard many life coaches tell audiences that they've made a fortune, gone bankrupt, made a fortune, gone bankrupt again, and made another fortune . . . as if anyone who really wants to enjoy great wealth has to suffer ruin and huge ups and downs financially. I don't think that's true at all, but it is true that you have to be willing to give it all up. The key to letting go of the fear that you could lose all you've worked for is to accept the truth that all the riches you haven't recognized or claimed in the past are still available to you. The door to abundance is never locked – it just sticks sometimes when you're not truly ready to receive wealth.

Action Steps to Tune into Abundance

To tap into the vibration of abundance, follow these simple steps:

∞ Write down your top goal on an index card. Carry it with you every day and read it many times throughout the day. Include emotionally charged words like:
  - "It feels great to own..."
  - "I am happy and grateful now that in an easy and relaxed way I am earning more than \$x,xxx,xxx a year."
  - "I am absolutely thrilled now that my personal net worth is in excess of \$x,xxx,xxx."
  - "I'm so happy now that I OWN outright my gorgeous home" (define the home if you know what you would like).
∞ Research online for success stories and read them to inspire you.
∞ Read magazines that share inspirational accounts of others' success.
∞ Read the *Early to Rise* newsletter when it arrives in your inbox every day. This newsletter is filled with brilliant ideas.

- ∞ Find stories of people who made a fortune online with one idea.
- ∞ Create a journal of "million-dollar ideas" and make entries every day. (Even if you only make one entry a day, eventually you will discover *your* million-dollar idea.)
- ∞ Make an investment in yourself – it is one of the wisest investments you will ever make!

Peggy McColl is a *New York Times* best-selling author and an internationally recognized expert in the area of goal achievement. With her goal achievement seminars, speaking engagements, audio programs, and best-selling books, she has been inspiring individuals, professional athletes, and organizations all over the world to realize their goals and reach their maximum potential. Find out more at http://www.destinies.com.

Aurea McGarry

Live Your Legacy

When the diagnosis is grim, keep expecting miracles...

What are you doing right now to live your legacy? Young or old, it is never too early or too late to take charge of your life and decide what it is you want to leave behind on this earth when you die. What will it say on your tombstone to sum up your life here on earth? What do you want people to remember about you?

Now, no one wants to think about dying, and as a cancer survivor myself, I don't either. It's funny what you do think about, though, when you get hit with a potentially life threatening illness that forces you to take a look at your own mortality. Even more difficult can be the reality of what you have or haven't done with your life thus far. Let's not think of dying – let's think of living. Let's focus on whether we are actually living our lives or just going through the motions of surviving our daily habits one day after another, never reaching out, never creating a legacy.

Twists and Turns

When I was diagnosed on my thirty-eighth birthday with non-Hodgkins lymphoma in the fall of 1999, I could honestly say that I was a fairly fulfilled woman up to that point. Of course, I had many unfulfilled dreams; after all, I was born and raised in New York City with aspirations of becoming a famous singer, dancer, and actress one day. But life takes its twist and turns, and we can sometimes be sidetracked, while discovering new dreams along the way. I had become the mother of a great little girl who was in eighth grade at the time. Angelica is a beautiful singer and musician herself, so her name fits her perfectly – she does sing like an angel.

I was happily married to my second husband, Brian, my prince charming. We had been married only three years when I received my cancer diagnosis. Never once did he leave my bedside. I had survived a domestic violence lifestyle several years earlier with my first husband, when I realized after seven years of abuse that life was too short and I had to move on or I would die, maybe not physically, but emotionally and spiritually. I was also a very successful entrepreneur with a large home-based cosmetic business. Life was good, and I had nothing to complain about.

During surgery to remove the cancerous tumor from my chest cavity, the doctors had to remove my thymus, where the cancer started, and half of my left lung along with part of my right lung. They also took out the lining around my heart and disconnected half of my diaphragm, telling me I would probably never hiccup again (something I was not too concerned about). The final cut removed the left thoracic nerve to my vocal chord.

In an instant, while I lay asleep, my life would change forever. As the doctors told me all of this when I woke up from surgery, with tubes coming out of too many places to mention, a memory flashed in my head of the day my father was murdered gangster-style, shot three times in the back of the head and left for dead on the side of a road on his birthday, many years ago when I was in high school. That infamous day, I went from being a multimillionaire's daughter to a high school girl with nothing financially. Life happens while you are making other plans, and I had experienced that a lot.

So when the doctors proceeded to tell me that I would never be able to speak above a faint whisper again, I knew I had to pray like never before. It was at that very moment in the ICU that I prayed to God to either please heal my voice so I could speak again despite the grim diagnosis or show me how to live an exceptional life without a voice. I told God that either way he would get the glory. At that moment the Lord spoke to my heart and told me that I was going to write a book that would assist many others. I was so excited at that moment that I knew everything was going to be all right somehow.

Over the next six months I had to undergo grueling chemotherapy treatments that made me so sick I had to be hospitalized after each one for five days. My voice did not work very well at this point, just like the doctors had said, but I was alive and on the road to recovery, which was more important to me than if I could talk loudly or not.

Time to Evaluate

When your life suddenly changes overnight in a dramatic way, you almost have to stop and evaluate what you are doing with the precious life that has been given to you. How fast it all can change or come to an end at any moment! It made me think of strange things like, *If I died today, who would be at my funeral? What would they be saying about me? Did I do a lot of good things in my community? Would people be sad to see me go? Will others miss me besides my family and friends? What will they write on my tombstone to sum up my life here on earth? I want to leave a legacy, but how?*

These thoughts have stayed in my mind ever since, and even while I was so sick during the treatments I woke up every day with such a new appreciation for God's very fragile gift of life. I focused on what memories I could make today with my family and friends. Never having said to my daughter that I was too busy to stop by school to have lunch with her, I became so thankful that my teenager still wanted to have lunch with me at school with her friends. A New Year's Eve kiss with my husband, or a birthday cake when I turned forty.... I was so glad to have made it to the big 4-0, while others complained about getting older with another wrinkle.

I began to look at older people in their late seventies and eighties and think to myself, *Wow, they made it!* I am excited to grow old now and become a senior citizen someday. I cherish every birthday and every wrinkle. (All right, I may start fighting the wrinkles!)

Dreams Come True

And then in the fall of 2007, my biography and self-help book became a reality to give others hope and inspiration since I am now cancer-free. My ultimate little girl dream is now coming full circle and coming true. I don't just want to grow old, I want to make a difference in a big way and leave this world a better place because I was here. My long lost dream of being on television and my new dream of living a legacy and assisting people are coming together for the first time. I am hosting my very own television talk show featuring people who are making this world a better place. Yes, a talk show! From being told I would never speak above a whisper again to God healing my voice well enough for me to speak to the world on stage and on television is a miracle in every way. A lifetime of dreams has all come true, better late than never (and never late in God's timing). *"Live your Legacy with Aurea McGarry"*, a television show that was a lifetime in the making, now spot lights non-profit organizations, their founders and selfless volunteers. Both get recognition and broadcasting time on a regular basis on my show that is dedicated to their journeys of hope and the lives they touch. I am so honored to share their legacies with you and to be living mine. Won't you join us?

Aurea McGarry was Mrs. U.S. Beauty of Georgia 2003. The author of her memoirs and self-help book "I Won't Survive, I'll Thrive!", Aurea is now living her dream as creator, producer, and host of the television show, "Live Your Legacy with Aurea McGarry". A sought-after speaker, she shares with women's groups how you can tell the size of the woman by the size of the obstacle it takes to stop her. For more information, go to www.aureamcgarry.com.

Manifest Success

David Neagle

What If You Did Forgive?

From the time we are born (and perhaps even before) we are exposed to many mistakes that people make that affect us either directly or indirectly. Sometimes those mistakes don't seem like mistakes at all, but rather things that are done to us on purpose – various acts of revenge, anger, sadness, or meanness. With each act, we define the meaning and emotionalize the content before storing it somewhere deep inside. Sometimes we say we can't or won't forgive because the pain is just too great. Maybe we were taught by our parents not to forgive or that forgiving is a sign of weakness. Whatever the reason, many of us don't forgive. Even more troubling, many of us simply don't know how.

I would like to give you a gift that just might be a turning point in your life, if you allow it. First, let me say that it is no accident you are reading this right now. There is a reason that you have come into contact with Debbi's book. In order for you to be able to receive this gift, I want to assist you to see things from a different point of view. Sometimes that's all it takes, just a different point of view, and you are set free.

Obstacles to Forgiveness

One of the biggest obstacles for you to break through around the topic of forgiveness is recognizing that whoever hurt you really didn't understand what they were doing when they committed the offense – even if that person was *you*. That's right – the person you must forgive the most might be yourself!

115

The difficulty in embracing the concept of forgiveness stems from what I call "incomplete knowledge." If a person is lost out in the wilderness with a map, that map will not do them any good if the person has no idea where he or she is in relation to that map. The map might be accurate down to the smallest detail, but it is useless because the person has "incomplete knowledge."

This is the very problem people experience with forgiveness. Forgiveness is the map that points the way to personal and emotional freedom, but we don't understand where we are in relation to it. We are lost in a wilderness of beliefs that create various emotional states because we look at our world through those filters. Beliefs cause us to see the world through very specific models. If you have a belief that a certain kind of person is bad based on their race or religion, you would subconsciously look for verification of that belief. Every time your mind found a match you would say, "See, it's true," thereby strengthening your belief. When you can't forgive, you keep creating more of the same model that represents the offense, and every time your subconscious recognizes that pattern it says, "See, it's true." If you are holding onto anger, you will always have verification of something to be angry about. If you are vengeful, you will always be a victim to verify your vengeful belief.

Each belief that tells you why you can't or shouldn't forgive is like a broken compass that can't point the way home. So where is home? To understand that, you must understand the essence of who and what you are. Your core essence is love, and it is important to understand that even the most despicable person you can possibly imagine is also love at their core. Now, if you have any other belief inside you at this moment, it will tell you that this can't possibly be true and then send up thoughts about various individuals that have done really terrible things to validate that belief. This is nothing more than a belief trying to control your reality.

What Are Health and Freedom Worth to You?

It can be very frightening to the average individual to even think of replacing beliefs that have protected them most of their lives. However, it's important that you release beliefs that don't serve you and replace them with those that do. If love is the foundation of who you are, you can easily begin to see how any belief that is out of harmony with love could not possibly serve you. This is where people develop a feeling of being lost internally. They know something is not right but don't know where to look because they don't understand the core of who they really are. Everything they understand about their world takes them further away from the truth they require in order for the map of forgiveness to work.

There's a difference between forgiveness and resentment, anger, shame, and guilt. Resentment, anger, shame, and guilt are states of mind you must hold onto in order for them to be effective in your lives. Each time you experience them, they cause you to feel bad and release harmful chemicals that are destructive to your body. You must constantly relive the events or circumstances that created these beliefs in order for you to justify these bad feelings. It spills over into every area of your life and can affect everything from your health and finances to your ability to have quality relationships with others.

These beliefs can consume you for a lifetime and will assist you in creating other negative beliefs to support the ones you have developed as foundation for survival. Ask yourself a question: "What would I be willing to pay for my health and freedom?" You can't put a monetary figure on this, but you give away both your health and your freedom when you refuse to forgive. Not forgiving does nothing to another person at all. It only harms YOU!

So, how *do* you forgive? The easiest way is to become aware that you have the ability to just "let go." If you were holding a burning hot rock in your hand, you wouldn't even have to think about dropping it – you would just do it because of the intense pain of continuing to hold it. In a

117

similar way, not forgiving causes intense pain, so all you are required to do is to drop it. "Let go and let God." It's that easy, and it's that simple. We all must learn to realize this fact. Christ taught that there was no hope of forgiveness for the unforgiving. The quality of your forgiveness should be as broad in scope as faith, love, and hope.

David Neagle is president of Life Is Now, Inc., a multimillion-dollar company dedicated to showing entrepreneurs how to use the power of their minds to rapidly create success in both business and personal arenas. Known as "THE Million-Dollar Income Acceleration Coach," he is the author of *Just Believe* and *The Art of Success*. David publishes a regular online newsletter filled with strategies for building wealth and creating an ideal life. Visit David at www.davidneagle.com.

Jayne Neagle

All Things Real
Were Once Imagined

Optimizing Your Creative Powers to Manifest Success

All things real were once imagined. It was someone's creative power that reached across to the unreal world of the imagination and invited a thought or idea to manifest in the real. Creativity is an inherent ability belonging to all of us. It is the power to tap into the unreal and bring forth the thoughts we desire to manifest into the real. Everything in your life today first existed in your imagination, and through your own creative abilities and powers you have guided them all into existence. Those who believe they have a lesser ability to do this than someone else is really just expressing their lack of skill in harnessing or directing their own power.

If the question can be asked, the answer must exist. To have asked a question is in itself an imaginative process. And, since history has proven to us that all things real were once imagined, the answer must exist. So, what do you do when you seem to be stuck in finding an answer, a solution, or the next idea that will propel your life to a new level? What do you do when you want to have a great idea? You stop trying and start letting. I like to imagine that ideas are free-spirited creatures that would prefer to find their way into this world by their own choosing rather than to have you attempt to capture them. After all, it is in their nature to seek manifestation, which can only come through the power of creativity. That being said, be sure to hold a true intention of manifesting the right ideas when they come. They'll be looking to connect with those most ready to do so.

A Visualization Technique

In the same way that science fiction has inspired the creation of very real technologies, you can use your imagination to inspire the creation of anything you want in your own life. I would like to share with you a very real and almost instinctual visualization technique that I have used in my own creative and intuitive process.

Visualize a stream of warm, gentle, flowing energy moving around you. The energy within this stream is that which has created all life, God. This stream contains all knowledge. It is permanently by your side and completely available to you at any time, for any reason. See yourself reaching up into this stream. Instantly upon touching it, the energy begins to move in and through you. As you become one with the stream, your thoughts intermingle with the infinite number of thoughts riding the current. With so much information available, you must now actuate your own creative power to sort through and connect with the answers you seek. In doing so, you can optimize this process by utilizing the following three key skills.

Three Key Skills to Optimize Your Creative Power

1. Have a clear question. In order for the question to be clear, you must know the purpose for the answer. For instance, if you are looking for a way to increase your income, make sure you know the true purpose behind why you desire to do this. That acknowledgement puts you in a state of vibration that will assist you to find the ideas that are already in a matching or harmonious vibration. In other words, you'll be opening the door to an idea that is already seeking to manifest through you. This is crucial, because you sometimes have your mind set to receive thoughts that are only within a certain parameter, when in reality, the solution may be completely outside of that.

Many years ago, I started a business conducting live seminars. As a new start-up, cash flow was incredibly tight. I was looking for a way to market and sell the next seminar, but all the venues I found required making deposits I didn't have. The moment I switched my attention from how to produce a live event to the real purpose behind what I was doing – assisting others to achieve more and continuing to design my own destiny, I immediately tuned into the other possibilities available. A few weeks later I launched a massive teleseminar on universal law, something practically unheard of at that time. We met for one hour per week for thirteen consecutive weeks via phone. I reached hundreds of global participants who would not have been able to attend a live event. It allowed teams of people located in different corners of the world to work collectively together. The feedback I received was tremendous and appreciative. My overhead was practically nonexistent, and this gave me more freedom and flexibility in raising my four children, who were still quite young at the time. It was not what I had been looking for, but it fulfilled my purpose and proved to be very successful.

2. Say "Yes" to the ideas and thoughts you receive. This process is very much like siphoning water through a hose. After the initial flow of water is started, the rest follows right along. The more you accept your creative thoughts, the more you will receive. This does not mean that you should act on every thought that crosses your mind. It means you accept each thought as a possibility, without applying any judgment whatsoever. You must remain completely emotionally detached from your ideas; simply observe and record them as they come. Once you emotionally attach to any one idea, you begin to vibrate in harmony with it, and this causes a very focused attraction to more ideas just like it. Only after evaluating which idea best fits your true purpose is it effective to become attached to it. Then, in a harmonious vibration and with laser-like focus, you can collect supporting ideas and thoughts. As you continue, you will find everything bonding together in a cohesive pattern that will form a complete and viable solution in harmony with your purpose.

3. Act on the ideas that are most in alignment with your purpose. Even if an idea seems incomplete or does not seem to be capable of leading you to the complete solution you desire, go ahead and start doing what you can. Again, like siphoning water, the more that you let out, the more that comes in. You want to create a flow in your stream – not a dam. Acting on an idea opens the door to receiving more. Remember, ideas are like free spirits seeking manifestation. They will continue to seek until they find someone willing to accept them. If you cannot or will not allow them to materialize through you, they will find someone who will.

Of course in truth, we are all a part of and divinely connected at all times to this stream of infinite knowledge. What we commonly call "being creative" is our own personal power to communicate with this stream. This visualization is simply a tool you can use to strengthen that power so you can be more creative than ever before. Once you have strengthened your own creativity, you will find this same visualization technique to be very powerful in assisting others to clarify and strengthen their thoughts and ideas during masterminding, brainstorming, or consulting sessions.

Jayne Neagle is the vice president of Life Is Now, Inc., a multimillion-dollar company dedicated to assisting entrepreneurs to use the power of their minds to rapidly create quantum leaps in both business and personal arenas. Highly regarded as a creative consultant and an entrepreneur, Jayne is also an award-winning writer and the author of *What Would I Say if I Had One More Day?* and coauthor of *Design Your Destiny*. Visit her at www.JayneNeagle.com.

Tamir Qadree

Your Ship Comes in Over a Don't Care Sea

Many times in my life I have been in desperate situations where I thought I "needed" some amount of money, or this car, or that career, only to be bitterly disappointed. For example, when I worked for corporate America back in the late 90s, I was always striving to be number one, to be the best. While that may sound noble, it was disheartening, discouraging, draining, and painful.

I put myself in all those desperate situations. Every month I sentenced myself to repeat the same madness that did not serve me in the first place. By the time that I was thirty-nine years old, I was worn out, drained. I was getting older, heavier, and had three more babies to support. That's when I started to investigate how I could live my calling, which I have known since before I was ten years old. I read books, listened to CD series, and went to seminars. I joined network marketing companies, always bitterly disappointed at the outcome. Nothing seemed to happen fast enough. It was just not enough, period.

Time was running out, and my wife was bewildered because she did not understand what was going on. People who "thought" they knew me were whispering words like, "Why doesn't he just get a regular job and stop dreaming?" Even my in-laws chimed in with their two cents.

The Game of Wealth

Then suddenly it happened! I had played a game I learned from Ester and Jerry Hicks. I put $2000 into an imaginary bank account; the idea was that I had to spend all of it the very next day, and then put the $2000 back plus $1000 more. I vowed to do this for one year. The amount of money would be astronomical after a year by adding an extra thousand per day.

That same day, a friend of mine called with a few questions. I told her that I was a life coach, and she said that she would like for me to coach her. I gave her the price of my coaching, which was exactly $2000. (I had not set a price for my coaching, and I did not have a schedule yet, but the number $2000 just came soaring out of my mouth.) She purchased my coaching services by credit card on the spot! I totally freaked out after we hung up! This was magical, mystical, and a big blessing considering that I was broke *(or at least I thought I was)*.

I had had a few coaching clients over the years (three to be exact), but I had never received $2000 for a single transaction at any time in my life, even when I sold cars. What happened? This was a lady that hadn't spoken to me in two years, would not return my phone calls or emails, and yet calls on the very day I initiate this game – and presto! Within five minutes, she was giving me her credit card. Since that day, nearly three years ago, I have never gone without, nor have I lacked any good thing! Money is the *easiest* thing I have ever manifested! It just comes to me with ease and delight.

The Law of Indifference

I learned the law of indifference, which simply says, "I don't care about the results." When I no longer labored, worried, and agonized over what I didn't have, the results showed up. I learned that I had been pushing too hard, straining and going against the natural order of life. Life wants to manifest all of your desires, but you must "let" it to "have" it! Many of you allow your ego to get in the way. When I learned to silence the ego's chatter, I began to lead a magical life.

When you no longer worry, when you stop caring about how, when, where, and who your manifestation of money, harmonious relationships, or whatever will come through, you allow the natural flow of life to bring it literally right to your doorstep. The famed law of attraction works best when there is no struggle, no grasping, and no whining about what you don't have.

When you are patient, indifferent, and calm, you are telling the universe, "I know that I already have what I have asked for." You then move about with confidence and poise, you give thanks and appreciation, and you show gratitude for having already received it. Then, to your amazement, IT SHOWS UP!

Forget about *when* it will manifest! Why should you care? That is not your department. Just as you would not dig up an appleseed that you planted yesterday to check on its growth today, you should not dig up your thought seed. Your faith (trust) in the working of universal law is the seed and sunshine of its nourishment and coming forth into physical reality. Learn to trust! Believe in your power to manifest.

What we envision, think, speak, and write will be manifested in the physical world every time. The key thing is to remain calm, relaxed, and patient – trust in the spiritual law of manifestation. Take this affirmation from Florence Scovel Shinn: "My ship comes in over a don't care sea." Say it, say it, say it, over and over until you feel it click within you.

The Law of Nonresistance

The great Nazarene said, "Anything you ask for, believe that you have already received it, and it will be yours." He did not say, "Anything that you ask for, and then worry and fret about will manifest." Worrying will only manifest more frustration, worry, and lack.

What we resist will always persist, and what we fight is only strengthened by our opposition. To stress and strain over anything is to invite more or the same into your experience. That is why the law of nonresistance is so vitally important.

Just imagine lifting weights in a gym. Resistance training creates speed, definition, and some power. When you resist a thing in the mental world, it enlarges and speeds up the process of what you resist. You actual strengthen the muscle of what you resist!

Instead, resist nothing. Relax, stay calm, be full of peace, and you *will* manifest abundance!

Peace, Abundance, Opulence, and Prosperity

Prosperity is connected to peace. A friend of mine always says, "Your peace is your power." Being at peace means being satisfied with your abundance *now*. It means being grateful to the great ALL THERE IS, or GOD, for your life. A good affirmation is: "I am satisfied with my rich, opulent, abundant prosperity, which from now on makes no time in delaying to please me."

This satisfaction is also connected to the "don't care" state of mind. Here you have taken the idea of "time" out of your manifestation. You leave the results to take care of themselves while you give thanks and show appreciation by doing some act that correlates with your declaration of trust or faith. This might mean leaving a side of your driveway clear and open for the new car that you will manifest.

The "Gap"

If you were to put your hands together (open palms as in prayer) and slowly pull them about five inches apart, you will notice that between your right hand and your left hand there is only empty space – a nothingness or a gap.

Imagine your right hand being what you desire and your left hand being the desired thing itself. The only difference between you having and not having your desire is an empty space. In other words, **"There is really *nothing* at all between you and your desire."** All hindrances are imagined. The gap or emptiness represents your doubts, fears, worries and anxieties. Once you move past those imagined barriers and produce trust, faith and peace of mind, you will manifest your desires.

Now, go and manifest another world for yourself and others to enjoy!

Tamir Qadree is a master of attraction. He has devoted his life to the study of human success and the powers of the mind and spirit. Through experience, Tamir realized that everything that we require to succeed in any endeavor is already within us; there is no "out there." Once Tamir realized this, his life and career started to flower; his desires began to manifest faster than he could imagine. Get 15 minutes "No Fee" coaching consultation and a 7 day trial membership to Esteem Live Worldwide Community by visiting www.esteemlive.com or email info@esteement.com.

My greatest and dearest prosperity gift from God, is the gift of my loving wife, Theresa Qadree.

Manifest Success

Randy "RD" Riccoboni

Drawn to Success

I am a self-taught artist who draws and paints the world I see. Being an artist is a blessing; it's a rewarding and fulfilling career. I am grateful that I can exercise my creative talents and bring joy to the people who see my art.

When I was five years old, I discovered my mother's paint-by-numbers set. It was a sailing scene of Old Ironsides –the U.S.S. Constitution. I was off and running, painting and drawing everything around me. In school, my favorite subjects quickly became Show and Tell and Art class. My parents were supportive of my artistic abilities, as it kept me quiet for hours. One day, my aunt brought me a book on the French Impressionist painters. I immediately started copying pictures from the book, happily making my own versions as gifts for my family. I boldly told everyone, "When I grow up, I'm going to be an artist!"

Artists often receive negative input from outside influences – well-meaning people who are stuck in the emotions of lack and drama. I was no exception. How many times have you heard the phrase "starving artist" or heard someone say, "An artist isn't taken seriously until he's dead"?

Over the years, waves of success came and went for me. I could never quite put my finger on why this happened. What caused it? It certainly could not be me! Perhaps it was the economy or the fashion of the time. Perhaps certain colors were in and others were out. It had to be an uncontrollable source outside of me, right? I seemed to be always swimming against the tide. After all, that was the life of an artist – struggle and sacrifice for art's sake in order to leave a legacy for the world, discovered and revered long after the fact.

A "Real" Job

Before long, as so many other budding artists do, I left the idea of being an artist behind. One day a distant relative had said to me, "An artist? That's crazy talk. Get a real job, be a banker – that's what your cousin is." Before I knew it, I was a banker, followed by careers in retail and human resources, with the thought of being an artist always haunting me in the pit of my stomach.

At work, my coworkers saw the gift I had, but I had lost sight of it through negative thinking. I'd be fuming to myself while decorating the company bulletin board, *Oh if people just knew what a wonderful artist I really was, I could leave this awful job; I'd show them!* Thriving on my inner drama, I never even heard the positive comments they said.

In the late 1980s my family and I had some serious financial mishaps. Bitter, disillusioned, and barely making ends meet, one day I received a solicitation from a large nonprofit asking for money for AIDS research, and it sent me over the edge. I wanted desperately to help and did not know how. You see, I had lost my home, almost all my friends, and many coworkers because of this terrible disease. Upon opening the letter, I thought, *I am so sick and tired of this dis-ease, but I have no money to assist…. What could I possibly do?* This little voice inside me said, "Paint, you can paint!" and that's exactly what I did. I got into action and began painting. This decision was a defining moment in my life. I started creating enough paintings for an exhibit with happy, upbeat, bright colors.

"You Can Paint!"

Soon word was out that I was an "artist." A friend offered his lovely home as a gallery for our fundraiser. We found more artists who wanted to be involved, we selected a worthy foundation, and we invited every person we knew. This became a group art exhibition, and it was a huge success! I discovered right then and there that I wanted to be a painter and assist others by using my talents.

I moved cross-country to California and continued to do work as an artist. Eventually I was represented by a world-class art museum, and a book of my artwork, *Rainbow Nation,* was published internationally.

I have traveled all around the country, signing books and meeting young artists who wanted to be like me someday! I've launched more shows, and I've served on the boards of local art organizations. One of the exhibits was recognized by the White House, and involved traveling to Washington, D.C., to show how art can bring awareness and community together on important healthcare issues.

However, I didn't continue to develop new goals and practice the positive thought processes I had stumbled upon. Without the proper tools to keep me going, I stalled. I bought back into the negative, "woe is me," poisonous thinking around me. Like a worn-out tire, eventually I blew out...literally. A physical injury threatened to end my career abruptly, which would cause me to become that suffering artist everyone warned me about! I required and desired a miracle!

Needing inspiration, I took myself to the bookstore. In the architecture section, I heard that familiar voice within tell me, "You can paint flowers," so off to the gardening section I went. Upon arriving there, BAM!, a book literally fell off the shelf and hit me in the head, landing right side up at my feet. The book was *The Artist's Way* by Julia Cameron, and it was the catalyst that got me back on track.

Attracting the Positive

I finally realized that I had to change my thinking! Because of my thoughts, I was attracting both negative and positive circumstances. Not knowing how to change, once again fate would have its way. A friend recommended the book *Healing Back Pain* by Dr. John E. Sarno, which gave me another concrete, powerful tool.

Putting little sticky notes around my house, car, and everywhere, I began telling myself that I was a healthy, happy artist; that what I do is draw and paint. Not realizing that I was affirming and visualizing, I began to see myself healing, creating beautiful art, surrounded by loving, appreciative friends and family, living abundantly with people from all over who enjoyed my creativity. I imagined how that would feel, and that *is* how it *really feels*, because it is the very life I live today. I took charge of rediscovering myself and my destiny.

With practice, an amazing shift in my thinking has occurred, along with the folks I'm attracting into my life. It's actually become difficult to have negative thoughts, and I am so grateful for that! One thing I have come to realize about changing my thinking habits is that even if I don't get it at first, it will eventually get me!

These days, setting goals and reaching them allows me to live a full life surrounded by wonderful, loving friends. I have my own business. I've opened a respected art gallery. I'm a published artist whose work is exhibited in business establishments and museum spaces. I share my story with groups of students, business professionals, and charitable organizations. Once again, that little boy is running around showing his pictures and telling stories!

We're never done, retired, or graduated, and that's what keeps life exciting! Joy is the success in the journey of life, not material things. You will attract those outside things – money, stuff, relationships – when you are joyous. Keeping our side of the street clean on this journey and inspiring others to reveal their success promotes more joy and more miracles. I have seen it in my own life and in the lives of others.

You *can* accomplish your desires and intentions with right thinking, self-responsibility, and right actions. You too can experience miracles, find your purpose and passion, and joyfully be drawn to success.

Self-taught California artist **Randy "RD" Riccoboni** is an entrepreneur and a visionary. Exhibited and collected internationally, this painter has created a successful art-based corporation, which assists others to promote their artistic passions and realize their true creative value. See his beautiful paintings at: http://Beacon-Artworks.com and Beacon Artworks Gallery, San Diego, California.

John and Linda Sener

Forever Has No Ending
...But It Has a Beginning

Manifesting a loving, healthy relationship that will last a lifetime begins with passion –passion for life, passion for growth, and a deep, abiding passion for commitment.

Our beginning was a picturesque July 4th, 1984. Sparkling fireworks streamed down and disappeared into Stillwater Cove just below the renowned Pebble Beach Golf Course. That was day one, our *beginning*. By saying yes to a drive around Carmel in a mutual friend's convertible and stopping for late night champagne as a summer rain fell, we set into motion a series of events that would eventually bring us to where we are today – writing this chapter together and celebrating twenty years of marriage. As synchronicity of the Universe would have it, our deadline for completion of this love letter falls fittingly on May Day, 2008, our twentieth anniversary.

Today we live in Santa Barbara, California, with twin teenage daughters. We are blessed to have lived in two world-class cities with paradise-like settings, which made romance easy in the early days despite the typical newlywed struggle to make ends meet. And now, two decades later, co-writing this chapter is a unique tribute to express the depths of our love and dedication to each other. With limited space to go into the details of the life we have created, we'll just say that each day brings high adventure, knitted together with the lowest of lows and sprinkled with an abundance of pure joy, laughter, tears, and gratitude for it all. Call us "romantics"; we don't mind!

135

The Measure of Success

What does it mean to be in a successful relationship? In business, success is measured by financial and fiscal numbers; in the business of relationships, the measurement of success is the quality of the life that is created. Webster's defines success as "the favorable or prosperous termination of attempts or endeavors," implying that success means that one has "arrived" somehow, and the journey is over, having reached a "prosperous termination" – not very romantic, and not very accurate either in terms of loving relationships. If we have learned anything in twenty years, it is that we most assuredly are on a lifelong voyage with no land in sight, and if eternity is the destination, then we have barely set sail.

On May 1, 1988, we dedicated ourselves fully to the vows that date back centuries; *"to love, honor and cherish"* (and we all know the rest). With every ounce of our being, we committed to work through everything the Universe would throw our way. To put it mildly, the Universe has been busy working overtime, tossing multitudes of obstacles and opportunities in our path and challenging our commitment around every corner. Sometimes the waters became stormy and dark and everything in our being was saying, "Turn this boat around, or I'm jumping ship!" – no different than anyone else with an ever-present fight-or-flight instinct! But we believe in staying present in the moment and making space to begin communicating, which in time brings healing and a moving forward together. Our commitment to work through each obstacle is stronger than the desire to give up because things get too hard.

We would occasionally find ourselves blurry-eyed at 2:00 a.m., hashing things out in fruitless and dramatic arguments because someone somewhere said, "Don't ever go to bed angry." Well, when you're in a lifelong relationship, you soon realize it is not worth losing valuable sleep just because you are in disagreement! With the distinct luxury of knowing neither of us is going anywhere, we usually agree to revisit the issue "tomorrow." Our beauty sleep is preserved, and hey, with our ages hovering on either side of fifty years, we need all the precious age-reducing sleep we can get!

Too often couples attempt to find something in their relationship that they cannot find in themselves. We have figured out that in seeking the ideal relationship, we are actually seeking a meaningful relationship with ourselves. A relationship, like a successful business, is a living partnership that takes work to maintain. Each partner needs time and space to grow and explore spiritually, intellectually, and independently of the other. Over the years, we have learned the importance of giving each other the space to explore, travel, or try out new ideas. Many couples try to live their lives for or through each other, but it is when they truly come to know themselves as individuals that it becomes possible to share their lives with each other. To "be" in a successful relationship means to first know what it is like to just "be" with oneself.

Partnering to Parent

The birth of our twin daughters brought the most profound changes and deep insights into our relationship. What a blessing it has been to tie our lives together in a deep and unique bond that will be a part of who we are for eternity. We, as a couple, are very passionate, involved, introspective, and philosophical, which can drive our teens crazy, but it keeps things interesting!

As their parents, we have always been honest with our daughters about everything, including the mistakes we have made along the way, and we have taught them to live by the golden rule. They are kind, active, and spiritual in every aspect of their lives, and today, at seventeen years old, our girls have manifested themselves right into two very independent, loving, and successful teenagers! They have had the gift of two parents who have not coddled them or hidden the truths of the real world from them. We have advised them since they were babies to trust their instincts and honor their intuition.

137

Having seen other marriages struggle or fail, we recognize how easy it is to sleepwalk through a relationship by being so focused on being parents that spouses lose themselves in the process. We are honored to see the sense of pride our daughters have in themselves. They are willing to succeed or fail, and they know the benefits of taking responsibility for their own experiences. We are very proud to have raised two beautiful and capable human beings. As they prepare to leave the nest, we as a couple greet our next adventure with great anticipation, for a new life awaits us as well. The gift we give our children is that of ourselves.

One Simple Choice

So how did we get from our beginning to the present? Our answer goes back to the simple words of our wedding vows. There is only one choice when life becomes difficult or the challenges seem too great. Keeping our eyes on our commitment and our vows means always keeping our hearts and minds pointed firmly and unwaveringly in the direction of forever. Our story is one of love and trust, and the belief that whatever is not in front of us right now is on the way. Forever has no end...but it most certainly has had a profound and joyous beginning for us. As we sail into the years ahead, we are eternally grateful for the love of our family and dear friends, and we dedicate our lives, our love, and our successes to our children, whose lives are just beginning.

A wife's postscript...

The gifts of my life are the kind, loving and supportive soul of my husband and the unconditional love of my children, who think that I'm a little silly and emotional at times! I am inspired by John's willingness to trust the Universe with great optimism and his ability to touch people's lives in so many ways. I have been honored and supported in every endeavor that I have ever explored. John is the risk taker, and I, the gentle voice of caution, assist us both to learn to balance the two! The past has been my teacher, the future is a gift, and I chose to live in this present moment because it is here now and alive with promise. Though our story has no ending, it most certainly has had many beginnings that have led me here, and I am forever grateful for the journey.

John A. Sener, a native of Santa Barbara, California is a top producing Real Estate Agent of twenty-three years in the prestigious Montecito offices of Village Properties, specializing in partnering with clients to create their desired lifestyle through sound real estate choices. **Linda Yost Sener** is a personal chef/life assistant and full-time mom. Their pursuits include travel and mentoring others through writing, coaching, and speaking. Visit them at www.johnsener.com, or email them at john@johnsener.com or linda@lindasener.com.

Manifest Success

Kathy Shepard

Knowing I Have Value
Just as I Am...

Be careful what you ask for, you just might get it!

Think about that...

What if you actually believed and started receiving what you really desired? This was an interesting question for me, and the answers led to me writing this book (me, the recovering drama queen!) to share my quest to keep from going over the edge and have a fabulous life in the center. Yet just recently I had to double-check my own reactions and emotions in achieving this.

Here's what happened. Even though I spent considerable time and effort to attend an event and actually spoke at it, I was not publicly acknowledged or thanked. Now, I know my value, and I know the value I brought to so many people. I also know what value I personally gained. But the old drama queen side of me would have gotten more and more upset and "guilted" someone to send out another corrected thank-you notice.

In reality, it was a good test of my ability to receive benefit in the moment and allow the energy to flow through me and around me to others without blocking it. This way, more people shared in the moment. I visualize being a rock in a river; instead of the water being blocked, it just flows around or over the rocks and actually creates a natural polish over time for those otherwise rough rocks.

I am thankful for the lessons I received and can share with others. I spend more and more time quickly reflecting on my feelings and emotions. I ask more probing questions about what I am going through and why. I question why I am feeling what I am feeling. I am more aware of my emotions and more in control of my feelings. Sometimes the answers do not come to me immediately, but they do eventually come. The more focus I put on them, the quicker I come to a solution.

The Power to Forgive

Forgiveness...what an amazing word and an even better way to live! I recently was given the book by Paul J. Meyer, *Forgiveness...the Ultimate Miracle*. This book points out that forgiveness is essential for our physical well-being, and any unwillingness to forgive (and to receive forgiveness) also negatively affects our mental, emotional, and spiritual lives. This also spills over to our financial world, because giving and receiving forgiveness is necessary for all of us to live in the reality of reciprocity.

As a drama queen, I had to step out of my familiar world of drama and reflect on what the play of my life had been. I sat back and learned to critique the show as an observer and then decided that I could stop the drama at any time; I could be the casting director and thank the other supporting members for their roles in my life. It is *my* play. I deserve to receive a new and better show, anytime I choose to.

This was a new concept for me, as a recovering drama queen – to accept responsibility for my actions and attract other people and events to complete the acts in my play over my lifetime so I learn and experience the lessons I require. I can choose to continue to perform the part of being a victim, who was always sick and was constantly addicted to the highs that getting attention draws and the lows of the pendulum swings...

OR…

I can calmly stand up, declare my choices, and invite only people that honor, support, and love me to participate in my play in a way that reflects my current world.

Imagine a play where you not only are the one writing it, but also starring in it, directing it, constantly casting and recasting the participants, and also able to sit in the best seat in the house to watch and live it! That feels like true peace. I aspired to be this woman in power that I am now becoming, and you can, too.

Bad Dreams or New Realities – You Get to Choose

This journey has been a horrible nightmare at times. But I know now that I have the power to either stay in a bad dream or choose to awaken and create a new reality. The past is gone; I don't have to forget, but if I choose to forgive and let go, then I will not be held in bondage to the trials of my old ways.

It has been very therapeutic to write about and relive parts of my life up to today. Instead of staying in patterns that have obviously been repeated multiple times, I've begun to create new behaviors leading to better patterns. It's very freeing to realize that my past does not determine my future. I can and will make daily interventions in this fabulous journey of life.

I can take a long, slow, deep breath and give a true sigh of thanks. And you can too! Just pause right now, close your eyes, take a nice, long, full, deep breath to center yourself, and remember that you live in the here and now. You can choose to be happy!

Choose to acknowledge that you are good enough just the way you are. Look into a full-length mirror and sincerely convince the image staring back that, "I am loved and lovable just the way I am. If I breathe, then I am me, and it's all okay!" If this is the basis and foundation of your core beliefs, then everything else is a bonus!

Just Imagine

What if all you have to do is to be still enough to listen to the answers you are seeking? What if you can receive everything you desire? What if you let go of how it shows up and in what form? I've discovered that my limited plans can be replaced by a higher script, one that is just waiting for me to acknowledge it!

I hope that by taking this journey with me you have reopened some places in your own life that may have been crying out to be healed, forgiven, and released. Whatever your path, I applaud you for your ability to be strong enough to visit some of those painful places and allow healing to occur.

This chapter is from Kathy's new book, *The Recovering Drama Queen: How to Keep from Going Over the Edge and Have a Fabulous Life in the Center!* You can find out the "rest of the story" by purchasing her book at most major bookstores, online, or by visiting her Web site directly.

Kathy Shepard grew up on a dairy farm in Vermont. She says she's from "the barnyard to the balcony" because she now lives in a condo overlooking the ocean in south Florida. Kathy started out in the nursing industry and has now entered the world of real estate investing, marketing, and education. Her mission is to create more "recovering drama queens" and in the process create outrageous financial rewards for all. You can contact Kathy by emailing Kathy@RecoveringDramaQueen.com or by visiting www.RecoveringDramaQueen.com.

Embracing the Duality of Your Higher Self and Your Ego Self

What is the meaning of life? That is the universal question. In actuality, the question that you truly want answered is, "What is *my* meaning in this life?

We often look to others to answer this question for us. We seem to think that we "don't know." In actuality, each of us "does know." The answer is embedded in us, in every fiber of our being. We had the answer even before we came to our bodies. We hold the answer within us. The question then becomes, "How do we retrieve this answer?"

We retrieve the answer by accepting and understanding that we have two parts within us, which I refer to as duality, better known as our higher self and our ego self.

Duality Defined

Understanding your own duality assists you to bring forth the awareness that in essence, you are here to fulfill your soul's progressions. What makes us unique is that we each have a different soul's journey that involves many life lessons. Your soul's journey is built on both your ego and your higher self. Just like we are each different, so are our ego traits, depending on our soul's journey. The level of understanding you have of your own duality and what you choose to learn in this lifetime form the basis of your ego traits.

The ego is with you in every decision you make, and it is just as strong as your higher self. Your biggest struggle is trying to separate the ego from yourself. Despite the fact that your ego is only attached to you on this earth plane, it is equally as important as your higher self. Your ego can be something quite positive. It is meant to enable you to fully experience your physical existence; without your ego you truly would not learn. Your body is a giant filter; you filter your lessons through both your ego and your higher self. Depending on your understanding of the process, you can either speed up or slow down your soul's mission.

In every decision you make in life, you can choose to come from your ego or your higher self. You'll tend to get two answers to every question, one that comes from the higher self (which always speaks first) and one from the ego, which speaks second. Then you make a choice on which to follow. It's a process that we all go through before making any decision, those as large as "What is my meaning?" to small ones like," What I am going to wear today?"

The higher self speaks directly, to the point, and is always calm, even when it is a warning. It is assertive and comforting at the same time. Some people may have a physical reaction such as lightness of heart, a sense of bliss, or true love and excitement. When it warns, you might feel almost robotic, and you don't panic. For example, you are in a rush one morning. You grab your coat and keys and rush out the door, jump into your car, and start the engine. The radio is on, and there are many distractions around. You look in your review mirror and start to go into reverse. A calm voice says to you in your head, "You didn't lock the door." Everything in that moment is quiet for a second. You ask yourself, "Did I lock the door?" You try to envision a replay of leaving the home. *Did I? Didn't I?* Your ego makes you indecisive. *I don't have time for this, blah, blah, blah...I'm going to be late,* and so on. Your ego distracts you. You feel that you must worry about the things you HAVE to do.

The higher self gives you guidance and lets you make your own decisions. This is the filter process; you are being given a choice. It would be in your best interest to stop and go check that door. Or you could choose to ignore it and go on with your day. Your higher self (your internal guidance) has done its job; it has given you guidance. Your ego distracted you; both have done their job and have given you the ability to choose – what some will call free will. This is how you learn. Your higher self looks out for your well-being and makes life easy. Your ego distracts you, makes you indecisive, makes you worry, and makes life seem hard.

Get to know the internal conversations you have with your ego and your higher self and try your best to come from that wonderful place of the higher self that is connected to God consciousness. That is truly how you are going to understand your meaning in life. The harder that you try to push the ego away, the stronger the internal fight. It has you where it wants you: making no decision at all, staying in that same energy, with no change.

Shaping Your Ego

You are an ever-changing being; you are not the same person you were a minute ago. You are continuously learning, whether your ego wants to admit it or not. Because you are always changing, you can change your thought processes by what I call shaping your ego. How do you shape your ego? You do so by calling yourself on it. The more that you call yourself on it, the louder your higher self gets. You have to work on it.

With my clients, I begin with a simple exercise. I ask them to look in the mirror and say to themselves, either out loud or silently, every morning after brushing their teeth: "Today I come from my higher self, not from my ego." I have them repeat this at least ten times. When you do this, you feel a shift in your chest area or the area of your belly button. It's an energy shift; you are affirming this to yourself. The key is making yourself believe that this is true. You have to affirm that your higher self is in control, not your earthbound Ego.

Your Soul's Journey

Once you start to get a hold of your own duality, the big questions you ask are, "What is my meaning, and what are the lessons for my soul's journey?" Reflect on your past. Don't go back there, just observe. What has been a repetitive situation in your dealings with others? Are you still in that cycle? Do you still attract the same situations? This is where you start. You must close one door in order to walk through another. You must come to a place of making a change, so that the Universe can usher in new beginnings.

When I observe my own past, I know that my life's journey is to write and coach others to find their life's meaning when they feel lost. As an example of truly understanding and fully living the struggle of duality, I can say I know my meaning. Through my filter process, I know that I am making decisions from my higher self and truly living out my life's purpose. Because I know my meaning, everyone in my life now and in the future assists me to fully live and learn my meaning in the context of my physical existence.

We are unique, but we require each other to live out our soul's journey. Please take a minute and thank everyone and everything that has been with you already during this lifetime. Express gratitude for both the positive and the negative, for you would not be where you are and where you will be without it. This is when you start to truly live.

Tara Taylor is an intuitive counselor who has studied extensively in this field. Tara is the founder of Whitelight Wellness, a holistic practice specializing in energy healing therapies and spiritual counseling. Tara is known for her intuitive abilities and has assisted clients worldwide by educating them on their duality and their soul's mission. You can reach Tara at www.whitelightwellness.com, email her at tara@whitelightwellness.com, or call her at 613-233-2227.

Tom Watson

Just Outside
Life Begins "Just Outside" the Comfort Zone

"Really?"

"Yes, really! Would you like to go?" I asked.

"Yes, I have been thinking about going....do you have tickets?"

I replied, "I have a VIP pass with your name on it!"

I didn't. Not in my hands. But I knew that I could manifest one. I had been learning a thing or two about manifestation.

Plus, the way she said "Really?" arrested me. One word, two syllables, quantum intention. She wanted to go to the Sony Open Golf Tournament here in Honolulu, and her ticket and companion had just shown up.

Where It All Begins

To say I had a VIP ticket for Moni at that moment put me outside my comfort zone, but just a little outside. I believe that when an opportunity to express faith presents itself, it creates that rare and exciting chance to go outside – just outside – your comfort zone. That's where life begins: "just outside" the comfort zone. And if you need further proof, just consider the birthing process. Truly, "just outside" is where it all begins! Just outside the womb, that is! I missed the birth of my first child, Saxon Leigh, but the first time I saw her face in the incubator, she was warm and comfy and on her belly. Rapid breathing…a life just begun. Sleeping, growing, and duplicating cells en route to adulthood…nineteen years ago!

My second daughter, Sarine, did not come into the world as peacefully. She was a strong baby, even in the second trimester. In fact, she had caused her mom to be hospitalized with extreme nausea caused by hyper-hormone activity. Yes, Sarine was alive and ready early. Her heartbeat was arrhythmic, so doctors decided to perform a C-section on August 7th, 1992, at 11:00 am. Life begins on O.R. schedules now, or so it seems!

I was there for this one, complete with scrubs and my VHS Daddy-Cam. They let me videotape the whole thing, which I couldn't do too well because the sight of the incision and the free flow of blood made me a little woozy. It's amazing that "life is in the blood," yet it has that effect on some people. I'm one of them. It was easier to watch through the one-inch viewfinder as I recorded Sarine's first venture "just outside" the womb. After the doctor lifted up a flap of skin, he reached in and pulled her right out into the world. Her first impression? "WHAAAAHHHH! WHAHHHHHHHH!!" Cold, bright, and strange. She was out of the womb, just outside her nine-month comfort zone. And she didn't like it…who could blame her?

I wonder how many times we get forced out of our comfort zones, and our tendency is to simply scream! "WHAAAAHHHH! WHAHHHHHHHH!!" Especially when the circumstance was unexpected, unwanted, and permanent. Things like divorce, a business failure, or the loss of a loved one can hurl us into the unknown as quickly as a C-section. But as adults, we are not supposed to whine, right? We are supposed to deal.

"No, it's okay! It's good for her to build those lungs and clear the fluids!" the nurse told me when I asked for a blanket to cover Sarine. By now, she was in an incubator; however, unlike Saxon sleeping soundly, Sarine continued to cry loudly as I stood over her in my blue scrubs and hairnet. I wanted to comfort her, as any daddy would, but all I could do was whisper soft reassurances. "It's okay…Daddy's here. I am here, baby, it's okay."

Suddenly, Sarine grabbed my index finger and squeezed it. She had found her first human connection just outside the womb. Just outside her comfort zone, one baby hand grabbed one big Daddy finger and started to settle down. The crying became a whimper, and she eventually got her blanket, looking like a little tapas tamale. And so I believe it is with God. While we lay frightened, scared, and cold, our Father watches over us with the exact same words: "It's okay, I am right here…shhhhh…peace, child." If we only have ears to hear....

We should remember that the crying does stop. But sometimes crying is just what we need to "clear our lungs" as we adjust to new circumstances and environments. And then we find they're not so bad, and we can conquer them with enough will to live "just outside."

How many times growing up have we had the chance to go outside our comfort zones? Think about our school days. What types of events caused us to go "just outside" back then? Maybe it was trying out for the school play, the glee club, or Little League. Were we put on the spot with all eyes watching? Were we forced outside our comfort zones in those days? Even when we were in high school, the first crush, the first dance, going off to college – haven't we been living outside the comfort zone all our lives? But what about "just outside?" There is the traditional "outside the comfort zone," of course. But the life that really gets lived goes even further outside.

The Power of Choice

There is so much beauty in the power of choice. We humans are the only species embedded with the privilege and power to choose. Just like God told the Israelites after liberating them from Egyptian slavery: "Choose life," we can also "choose life" in our many daily decisions. One could argue that "choose life" means "choose to live." So many people are *choosing to exist* as opposed to *choosing to live*. Choosing to live means choosing to risk.

Flashback to Y2K. Hey, Hey, Hey! The year 2000 – that was a nice even number for a soul born in 1960. It was 2000 and I was approaching the big Four-O! I had set a goal with all my heart to be "retired" by age 40. A ten-year plan to earn $10,000 per month, which I laughingly thought would be enough to "exist." Sounds reasonable? However, I was a young married man, with two daughters, a mortgage, and all the trappings of corporate success. With intense sales and management positions, I pursued my dream: $10k per month in passive, residual income. I tried a lot of things. None succeeded dramatically, but I got the discipline of trying a few new things. I learned to get out of my comfort zone.

As entrepreneurs, we are a funny breed. It's almost like we are the 6 percent that can't hold a job, so we create jobs for the other 94 percent. Entrepreneurs truly live "just outside" every day. A dream will push us out of our comfort zones. If the dream is clear enough and important enough, it will push us to break out and give it a go. A dream will push you out of your comfort zone, but it's real friends who will pull you through. A true friend will cheer you on and challenge you. Any friend who does this for you already lives just outside their own comfort zones. That's why they are comfortable to exhort you to press on. They get it. They know the joy of achieving "just outside" accomplishments.

Here's the Drill

Whether it's believing you can build a business or believing you can come up with a V.I.P. pass for the Sony Open for a new client, the drill is the same:

"Am I willing to step out in faith to declare something?"

"Am I willing to act on it to bring it to pass?"

"Am I willing to leave the predictable to go just outside and take a chance?"

All great achievement is the result of a soul or a team of souls deciding to go outside the norm to create life. When we choose to stretch that comfort zone, we honestly do choose life. And all of life really begins where the adrenaline kicks in…just outside the comfort zone!

Tom Watson lives in Honolulu, Hawaii and is a full time network marketer. His career began in advertising sales in New York City in 1982. Tom held various advertising sales, marketing and management positions before going full time entrepreneur in 2000. He received a Top 5 Coach Award with SendOutCards.com in 2007 and then became one of the fastest certifying reps for Nouveau Riche. Tom can be reached at either www.nruhnl.com or www.sendoutcardshawaii.com, directly at 808 386 8295.

Manifest Success

Sharon Wilson

The Power of Prayer in a Healing Crisis

Imagine feeling wonderful, your whole life on track, and then, a routine physical changes all that. What if you were suddenly faced with a major health issue today? What if you discover that something is very wrong and requires immediate surgery?

In that critical moment, you face a healing crisis that will affect you forever. Such a crisis appeared in my life shortly after my "too-young-to-die" mother died. Her premature death did not scare me, because I take care of myself. I even go to extremes (according to family), and as a life coach I train others to use energy management and self-coaching processes to live more effectively.

Heading a successful organization that trains entrepreneurs to use an inner and outer approach to building and maintaining successful careers provides great income and a balanced life for me as wife and mother. I had everything I ever wanted, and then suddenly I needed two major surgeries. I was facing a possible malignancy and would require months to recover from such drastic intervention. I didn't know what to do.

First, I called both doctors involved in the surgery and then my spiritual mentor of many years to see what could be done to heal my body immediately. She assured me she had seen others healed to the extent that their physician's doubted their diagnosis. I wanted that to happen to me! I wanted it fast! I had a huge training schedule and joint ventures that required my presence, and I was scheduled for a spiritual retreat. I did not want to cancel my life or miss going to Ecuador with Ruth Lee, so we began working immediately.

Taking Inventory

How could anything this bad happen without any warning? Did I do this to myself? I was urged to review what produced stress in my life in recent years, and I discovered that I had buried a lot of personal grief while assisting others. I had ignored and denied that anything could be wrong, but now I recognized how much had been closeted and shut away to be worried about another day.

My inventory of stress-inducing events started with the death of my father-in-law, closely followed by the death of my beloved younger brother. I was heartbroken and in shock as I dealt with these deaths, but I never doubted that I took it all in stride and handled it well. Not long afterwards, I sponsored a spiritual retreat with my mentor, Ruth Lee, in Mexico. The first day away, news came that my trusted and much-admired business partner waited for me to leave the country to announce that she was no longer in business with me! Honestly, this hurt as much as if she had died! I tried to deny her hatred, but I could no longer ignore it. Thank God, both Ruth and my sister were there to counsel me. A few months later, my mother's health declined, and she began a long, terrifying fight for life that lasted almost a year. The last six months included many surgeries. She was barely sixty years old when she died.

Taking an inventory of these stress-inducing events assisted me to realize that my body had been talking to me, but I had ignored it. I now marvel that I listened when Ruth told me to seek a woman doctor immediately because something was wrong. I heeded her advice, even though I had been recently assured everything was fine.

My new woman doctor ordered a few tests and quickly detected a very serious problem in my reproductive organs, so serious that I needed a hysterectomy. During a colonoscopy, polyps were removed, and the surgeon, also a woman, said abdominal surgery was required to remove a large lesion. Just like that – two major operations with estimated ICU recovery time of four days and eight weeks' recovery afterwards.

Harnessing the Energies of Mind and Spirit

Wrestling with my belief in the power of prayer versus hard medical conclusions that nothing was about to go away without radical surgery, I fully embraced what I had done in the past and was guided to now activate, through a final attempt through prayer, all the energies of my mind and spirit to heal my body.

I have no intention of changing anyone else's mind about spiritual healing or the power of prayer. I am merely confirming that I am here today because I believe and will always believe that God stepped in and took over my life and healed my body right then and there.

Ruth Lee had worked with me for many years, assisting me with overcoming crises and turning them into opportunities. Known as a spiritual channel of healing energies, she came through for me and provided very specific information relative to my personal healing. Nothing prescribed in Spirit was difficult to understand or follow, but most might wonder how such simple things could heal anyone, let alone someone scheduled for two major surgeries in two weeks.

What I am sharing with you is what I was guided to do – each person is different, so you will have to follow your own inner guidance. I share with you what I did to explain just how simple healing can be when you pray and believe in God.

My "Prescription"

First, I drank a gallon of red raspberry tea every day! Ruth told me this would strengthen my reproductive organs and shrink tumors and fibroids. I still drink this tea.

Second, I concentrated on deep-breathing exercises designed to oxygenate and promote cellular healing. I used Ruth Lee's powerful *Healing Breath* tape. After only twenty minutes a day, I could breathe more effectively, especially when combined with chanting the ancient Tibetan "Om, Mani Padme" prayer afterwards.

Third, I continued using yogic exercises designed to allow my chakras to align. There are seven spinning energy vortexes (chakras) in the body that regulate bodily functions. When you are stressed, they spin unevenly and disrupt your physical well-being.

My surgeons allowed me time to get my business in order and work with this healing program. These seemingly easy tasks produced good news from my gynecologist! She discovered there was no need for a hysterectomy; the tumor had shrunk and no longer warranted surgery. As far as I am concerned, powerful prayer, the raspberry tea, and my deep breathing saved the day. The general surgeon then agreed to give me another colonoscopy the day before my scheduled surgery to insure that I still required it. I am so grateful to have doctors who believe that miracles are possible!

In the short time that I worked on my personal healing, I started taking rutin, as Ruth advised. I also used a self-coaching process in my daily routine. I followed what I teach in my coaching programs – managing energy moment-by-moment. Much can be accomplished during mediation when using visualization, but if you return to the same thought patterns, you don't get immediate results. You must consistently follow a process that enables you to shift your beliefs and erase old patterns that no longer work.

Prayer Is Powerful!

The day before my surgery was scheduled, I accepted it if this last-minute colonoscopy revealed no improvement. After the test, my surgeon approached me in recovery and said, "I got it all, Sharon! It's gone, and I'm canceling your surgery!" – just as I had visualized day after day as I meditated and prayed. As she walked away, my surgeon gave me a huge smile and said, "You're the talk of my office! Nothing like this has ever happened before." I replied, "I have visualized you saying this so many times, and now it's true! Are you sure I'm not still under anesthesia?"

I was so happy! I asked Jesus and all those working with me to assist others facing illness of any kind to feel this same joy and to feel safe and at peace like me. I sent this message to everyone, and I am sending it to you now!

All happened just the way I had seen and felt over and over again in my daily prayer and healing intention sessions. I will never again doubt the power of prayer, and I have rededicated my work to activating this healing energy in others. Prayer is powerful! Prayer is *your* connection to God and to all the energies that heal and support each of us. Prayer is the answer! Not random prayers of supplication, but intentional prayers directed at the cocreation of our lives.

As for me, *I am convinced* that prayer heals! I believe we are meant to pray with our bodies – not just for them. See your body and its energy flow through you as a healing wave when you pray and meditate.

Sharon Wilson is an author, certified spiritual counselor, and founder and chief inspiration officer at the Coaching from Spirit Institute. Sharon healed herself in forty-five days from being scheduled for not one but two major surgeries. Go to www.coachingfromspirit.com/healing for more resources. As her gift you will also get *Success Through Your Spirit - The Golden Six-Figure Formula* ($79 Value) AND free admission to *The Missing Link to Your Entrepreneurial Success* and *Top Secrets to Becoming a Spiritual Life Coach* LIVE teleclasses (a $78 value).

About the Author

Debbi Chambers is the creator of the award receiving "Manifesting Garden-Create Your Garden of Infinite Possibilities, A 45 Day Goal Achievement Adventure. Debbi assists her clients in not only setting their goals, but also creating successful results. Her satisfied clients lovingly call her the 'Manifesting Muse'.

She recently launched her new company, Rhino In Pearls, an online oasis of self empowerment information, business tips and wealth co-creation (affiliate) projects. www.rhinoinpearls.com

Together with her 'Web Success Diva', Maria Reyes-McDavis, Debbi created the wildly successful Network Marketing Success 2.0 System. In their easy to follow, step by step videos, they share Internet Marketing Strategies and Network Millionaire Mindset™ to attract qualified prospects and clients. Take your income and your business to the next level, visit www.networkmarketing20system.com to receive your free Viral Marketing instructional video

Manifest Success

Manifest Success

Manifest Success